:

Psychotherapy
In Ordinary Language

by
Richard Driscoll, Ph.D.

Psychotherapy in Ordinary Language:

Create Space Edition November 2016

Copyright © 2012 by Richard Driscoll

Published by Westside Psychology at Create Space

ISBN-13: 978-1519675866

ISBN-10: 1519675860

Acknowledgements

Much of the material here is based on the work of the late Peter Ossorio at the University of Colorado at Boulder. I attended my first seminar with Ossorio in my first year in graduate school, in 1968, and continued to learn from him after that.

I think it is fair to say that Ossorio has crafted one of the most intuitively sensible formulations of psychotherapy available anywhere. Ossorio was gifted in presenting his material to classes, and a small community of former students are organized to continue his traditions.

Ossorio was also highly precise in his writing and therefore not easy for first time initiates to follow. I reworked a course transcript, and later expanded it to include most of his main points.

Ossorio had a way of making his material so sensible that it becomes obvious, once you see it, making it hard to know what to attribute. Which parts are from Ossorio, which are just common sense, which are from ordinary language analysis, and which are my own innovations? I provided citations for the most obvious particulars, and we invited his former students to scout for anything else which should be attributed.

I gratefully acknowledge Peter G. Ossorio for many of the particulars here and for the general sensibleness that runs throughout the material.

Table of Contents

Preface 1

Part I   Shared Concepts 2

1 The Promise of Ordinary Language 3

2 Multiple Facets of Human Action 12

3   Explanations of Behavior 25

4 Psychological Problems and Psychotherapy 43

Part II Guidelines for Interventions 58

5 The Therapeutic Relationship 59

6 Affirmation and Accreditation 89

7 Assessment 122

8 Clarifications 144

9 Ways and Means 160

10 Instill New Patterns 169

11 Motivations 182

12 Synthesis 201

References 208

Footnotes 213

Preface

A movement toward integration was well underway in the 1980's but now, more than a generation later, we still need a sensible way to organize our multiple approaches to therapeutic practice.

My aim here is to show how we can see farther and communicate more clearly with some assistance from ordinary language and a liberal smattering of common sense. One reviewer was especially impressed with the common sense quality:

"...there is so much common sense in this book that it borders on wisdom"
-- Gerard Egan, Ph.D., Loyola University, SEPI review of 1st printing

Part I
Shared Concepts

1
The Promise of Ordinary Language

Our challenge is to clarify what successful therapists do so we might figure out how to do it ourselves and then perhaps to improve upon it. You will find herein a practical way to do that. Much of the material here will be familiar, only better organized. Yet you will also find here a few absolute gems, unfamiliar to most clinicians and yet immensely practical.

A first is from Peter Ossorio at the University of Colorado, who suggests that we "Legitimize," or "Show the client the sense he or she makes." So we affirm the ways our clients are rational and sensible and understandable, and use that as an overview for showing how they are also mistaken or misguided. Suppose an individual uses the "always" and "never" superlatives in arguments with a spouse. We could simply say that she should not use "always" or "never," that it has a jarring impact, and then suggest she change. But why is she doing it in the first place? Suppose the woman tells her husband that he never talks about his feelings: We would do well to begin by legitimizing her actions. "You use 'always' or 'never' to make your argument sound stronger, and more convincing. That's understandable." And from there, we show why it fails. "While it seems stronger to you, your husband knows it is an exaggeration and feels it is unjust and untrue. So instead of listening to you, he argues against you, or maybe just ignores you." And from there, we suggest the change. "Actually, the softer argument often gets a better response. Try saying, 'You seldom talk about yourself;' or even better, 'I want you to talk about yourself more often.'"

By showing our clients the sense they make, we affirm their fundamental rationality. Amid the ways an action makes sense, the specific mistakes are clearer and easier to understand. As we continue to legitimize, as a matter of policy, we will see how human actions make better sense than we might have ever thought possible.

A second gem comes right out of ordinary language. In inadvertent actions, we act to attain one end but end up with another, quite unwanted, and cannot figure out what is going wrong. We will see here that much of what goes wrong with troubled individuals involves just such inadvertent acts. Clients want reasonable things and yet act in ways that get them unsatisfactory outcomes and further problems. The concept of "inadvertent" action and "unintended" outcomes make understandable one maladaptive action after another. I know of no other orientation that is explicit about inadvertent actions or that attends to them sufficiently.

In the illustration above the client uses the "always" and "never" words as a way to make the argument stronger, but inadvertently provokes opposition rather than understanding and compliance. Inadvertent outcomes are a trademark of troubled individuals, and we intervene to help clients get more of what they want and less of what they do not want.

Eclecticism and Integration. Older and more senior clinicians are more eclectic than beginners, suggesting that greater breadth and diversity of practice comes with experience.[1] A thriving workshops industry provides new and interesting tactics for clinical problems, and even therapists who do identify with a single theoretical orientation borrow components from elsewhere.[2]

The choice for eclecticism is obvious. A wide variety of insights and techniques are currently available, many of them commonly associated with one or another of the hundreds of schools of psychotherapy.[3] Interventions from one school may work best in some situations, while those from other schools are better in other circumstances. The appropriateness of any insight or intervention is due not to its school of psychotherapy, but to its fittingness to the particular problems of the case at hand. A working familiarity with several schools

4

allows us to choose from the best of what is available and to tailor it to needs of our individual clients

Yet the schools of therapy do not themselves provide adequate guidelines for when to use their methods and when not to. So eclectics use their own experience and common sense, which is usually adequate in practice but is hard to pass on to the next generation.

The original promise, mostly forgotten, was that a theoretical framework could be found which would nicely organize and the full range of behavioral concerns. The promise faded, of course, as each new framework proved inadequate to the job.[4] Our current therapies are becoming more practical and less theoretical, more observational and less speculative. Something about the theoretical paradigm leads us down the wrong path, and those old formulations of old are being abandoned and replaced with more straightforward and more practical alternatives. What is it we use now?

Ordinary Language Is Our Common Language

Experienced therapists function in an intuitive and commonsense manner, and are often unable to provide any theoretical justifications for what we are doing.[5] Our therapeutic proficiencies emerge largely from everyday good sense and social competencies, which we augment and improve upon by training and practical experience. Theoretical formulations may be blended into our existing know how about people, but do not overturn and replace our competencies and they are surely not the origins of social savvy.[6] Any satisfactory explanation must take our existing social hello into account.

Successful integration requires a common language that can be used across therapeutic orientations. Currently, each theoretical formulation uses its own theoretical concepts and terms, which produce its own separate language. Indeed, it is easy to identify any orientation by its commonly used words: The "unconscious" points to a psychoanalytic or dynamic orientation, "reinforcement" means you are behavioral, "self-concept" was introduced by humanists, "game" says transactional analysis, and so on. The presence of multiple languages among psychotherapists invites misunderstanding and confusion, reminiscent of the tower of Babel that failed for lack of a common tongue. It is an unusually acrobatic mind that can leap from one language to another without losing its bearings. Sadly, the findings from within any of the theoretical orientation are lost to those unversed in its language.[7]

A 1988 survey of integrationists listed the absence of a common language as one of the main obstacles to psychotherapy integration.[8,9] A NIMH workshop in the same year concluded that the single most important step in advancing psychotherapy integration is to develop a common language, and suggested that our everyday English language has the best chance.[10] And ordinary language is probably closest to what most therapists use already. In one clinic with a broadly eclectic orientation, practitioners were found to rely heavily on ordinary language concepts in their communication with their clients and with other clinicians.[11] New theoretical concepts and language conventions are rarely in the social sciences, and do not produce the same integrative solutions as those in the natural sciences.

Why so many languages? The new languages grew out of an early prejudice against ordinary language, which was considered too imprecise and too mundane for serious science. As popular champion of the prevailing view, B.F. Skinner faults our common vocabulary:

"The vernacular is clumsy and obese; its terms overlap each other, draw unnecessary or unreal distinctions, and are far from being the most convenient in dealing with the data."[12]

Beginning with Sigmund Freud and continuing through each subsequent theorist, the leaders of our field closed their minds and turned their backs to ordinary language as they raced to formulate the new and purportedly more scientific languages of their theoretical leanings.

Those who investigate ordinary language give us a much cheerier opinion of its practicality. Austin extols it breadth and versatility:

"Our common stock of words embodies all the distinctions men have found worth drawing, and the connections they have found worth making, in the lifetimes of many generations; these surely are likely to be more numerous, more sound, since they have stood up to the long test of the survival of the fittest, and more subtle, at least in all ordinary and reasonably practical matters, than any that you or I are likely to think up in our a armchairs in an afternoon—the most favored method."13

Our natural language is especially rich in its coverage of human actions, mental and emotional states, personality characteristics, relationships, and families and communities, which are on the short list of our usual daily concerns. We shall see how ordinary language concepts are particularly well suited to organize and clarify the shared concerns of practicing psychotherapists.

The most familiar ordinary language philosophers are Ludwig Wittgenstein and Noam Chomsky. Ordinary language psychologists include Fritz Heider,14 with "folk" psychology, and Peter Ossorio,15 who has introduced a "descriptive" approach. More recently, Steven Pinker uses the term "intuitive" psychology as he investigates how the mind processes information.16

Common Sense is Sufficiently Sensible

Common sense is in close alliance with ordinary language. Any scientific inquiry accepts the empiricist principle, stated thus: "We know about the real world by observation (and thought)."17 We need not observe everything for ourselves, but

7

observation is the final justification for what we might properly claim to know about the world. So where does common sense fit in?

The early traditions in psychology have been critical of common sense, promoting themselves as an alternative the mundane and unscientific opinions of the common man. Disparaging common sense, introductory texts juxtapose contradictory sayings such as "absence makes the heart grow fonder" versus "out of sight, out of mind," or "birds of a feather flock together" as opposed to "opposites attract."[18] Skinner contends that the old commonsensical ways of thinking about behavior is the main obstacle to the promising scientific alternative.[19]

The old theoretical psychology has a fondness for that which runs contrary to our ordinary ways of thinking.[20] "The successful theorist must develop a dispassionate willingness to do radical violence to common assumptions concerning behavior," and should be "freed from obligation to justify theoretical formulations that depart from normative or customary views of behavior," according to Hall and Lindsay's once popular *Theories of Personality*.[21] As Fritz Heider notes, "An assertion of a tendency contrary to the obvious... is felt to be a paradox, and often... imports a sense of great psychological profundity."[22]

The observation that some things are done on purpose and others are by accident or otherwise inadvertent is commonsensical and hardly qualifies as theoretical in the usual sense of the word. But Freud's famous claim that "nothing happens by chance" is a clever violation of our everyday experience, and suggests a theoretical importance far beyond ordinary common sense.

Freud's claim is a bold violation, but not a harmless one. This particular violation commands us to turn a blind eye to the inadvertent and the accidental, which are everywhere. Troubled individuals misunderstand how to act to their own advantage and so create further problems for themselves, inadvertently of course and not on purpose at all.

So long as the prevailing standards required something theoretical, the emphasis was naturally on the counterintuitive and against the commonsensical. The many languages of theories contribute to the flavor, recasting even the most commonplace observations in an unfamiliar light.

Yet certainly, given our years of human interactions, unless we are dimwits or simply wired incorrectly, we will have acquired a treasure chest of experience about the nature of our fellow human beings. How can all this be sensibly ignored? "The difficulty about developing a science of psychology is that ... we already know too much about human behavior. ... Common-sense... has creamed off most of the vital distinctions." [23]

Senior mathematicians and physicists have had a warm affection for common sense. "Science is rooted in... the whole apparatus of common sense thought" according to mathematician and philosopher Alfred North Whitehead. "You may polish up common sense, you may contradict it in detail, you may surprise it. But ultimately, your whole job is to satisfy it." [24] Did everyone follow that? The aim of proper inquiry is to *satisfy* common sense. "All sciences arise as refinements, corrections, and adaptations of common sense," according to physicist J. Robert Oppenheimer. [25] And similarly, from Albert Einstein, "The whole of science is nothing but a refinement of everyday thinking." [26]

Contrasts between the psychology and physics are remarkable, especially since early psychologists tried to pattern themselves after physics but missed the sensibleness of the inquiry. [27, 28] Physics is comfortable with ordinary language words, such as weight, speed, time, and so on, and introduces new words only when no familiar words are available. And physicists go to considerable length to make the world appear as sensible as possible. [29] For instance, that a two pound lead weight falls at the same rate as a one pound weight may seem odd at first but can be shown to be commonsensical: Since two one pound weights fall at the same rate, you can place them together, which does not alter their rate of fall, so that the two pounds together must fall at the same rate as either pound separately.

The common sense approach of the physicists is not the opinion of the man on the street, who has little opinion about physics anyway. The appeal is not in the commonness, but in the sensibleness. Common sense refers to a good fit between a proposition and the rest of our understanding of our world, so that the proposition seems to have an intellectually and aesthetically pleasing sense of being so. Common sense stands in contrast to that which is paradoxical, odd, highly speculative, unnecessarily theoretical, and otherwise counterintuitive and contrary to how we would judge things to be.

Common sense gives the benefit of the doubt to that which appears so over that which is counterintuitive. Stated as an axiom, "We take things to be as they appear, unless we have reason to believe otherwise."[30]

The point is not that appearances are always correct, but that they are the best place to begin. So those who argue against the way things appear must bear the burden of proof, to show how and why the new position is so. And if, in the light of further considerations, the appearance of the thing changes, then it is the alternative that appears correct and should be accepted.

We should try to explain assertions which appear puzzling, but we cannot be required to waste our time trying to explain everything. Common sense avoids the "never sure of anything" and the "how can we ever know anything, really?" binds of the philosophical positivists.[31] Skepticism carried to an extreme is not a quest for truth but a rejection of the practical commonsense requirements for negotiating and agreeing on what is and is not so. So common sense accepts things the way they appear, changes its mind after good arguments to the contrary, and allows us to just get on with things. Advances in psychotherapy can proceed by the refinements, corrections, and adaptations of our commonsense viewpoints.

Ordinary language and common sense produce unusual organization and clarity. Hidden nonsense becomes manifest nonsense, odd wording seems odd, the obvious looks obvious, good sense sparkles, and the few real innovations stand apart.

We use ordinary language concepts to organize and clarify the observables, and guidelines to specify the important tasks of therapy and organize the interventions.

2
Multiple Facets of Human Action

Brittany is out late, partying with her friends. She turns her key, opens the door, and softly tippy toes into the house and toward her bedroom. Surprise! The lights burst on and mom stands in the hallway, glaring at her. Caught! "Why do you always want to hurt me like this?" Mom demands.

So, what's going on? Most of us would suspect that mom is being somehow underhanded or manipulative. But why? What do we recognize that makes us suspect mom?

Look with her comment, "Why do you want to hurt me like this?" What does it mean by "want" to do something? Does Brittany really want to hurt her mom? Is she staying out late "in order to" hurt her mom or "as a way" to hurt her mom? Maybe, but that would hardly be her main reason. So far as Brittany is an ordinary teenager, we might more realistically suppose that she loves to party, as many teenagers do, and she is staying out late for the fun of it and to be with her friends, or perhaps to hang with a boyfriend. Perhaps that she stays out as a way to buck her mom and so assert her independence, or perhaps to be away from the house and away from mom. Brittany may be inclined to hurt mom, so far as she is angry at her, but that would hardly be the main reason for staying. So presume here that she is staying out late for the normal reasons, but in so doing she inadvertently hurts her mom.

What do we make of what mom says? Is mom really asking a question? Most of us would figure that it is an accusation, merely posing as a question. Mom is accusing Brittany of staying out late to hurt her, as a way to shame Brittany for her misbehavior and to call her to task. So mom accuses Brittany of being not just wrong, for staying out late, but maliciously wrong, for doing it as a way to hurt her. We might reasonably figure that mom "knows how" to confuse and manipulate, and is doing so to punish her daughter and to win the confrontation.

We are able to understand the incident here, including the confusion and manipulation, because we already have an intuitive grasp of these things. I outline here our shared concept, to gain a cleaner look at what goes on.

To understand our shared concept of human action, we begin with a most complete and understandable version, which is termed a paradigm case or model case,[32'] and then branch out from there. A complete and most understandable automobile, for instance, is one which runs, for it is through experiences with those which do run that we understand autos as vehicles of transportation. Autos which do not run are incomplete or failed cases.

The complete and most understandable case of behavior is intentional action.[33]

Intentional Action

If Brittany is hurting mom on purpose, then she "wants" to hurt her, she "knows" or believes mom is up and will catch her sneaking in, and she "knows how" to yank mom's chain. But if Brittany merely wants to be with her friends and was not considering her mom, or did not figure mom would catch her, or figures mom is just being dramatic, then it is unintentional.

So in an intentional action you know something about the situation, you want the outcome, and you know how to make it happen. You also perform the physical act, and achieve the results you want. The diamond schematic was introduced by Peter Ossorio[34] to show the relatedness of these parameters.

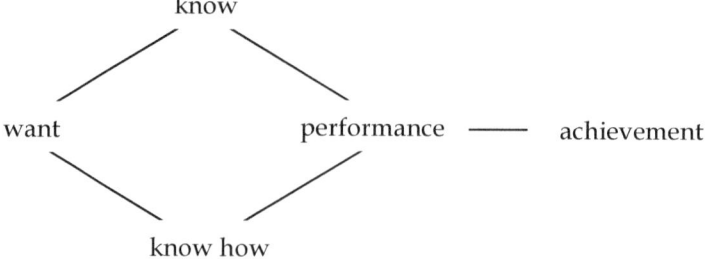

Figure 1: Facets of Intentional Action

At the risk of being too obvious, suppose you step on my foot. If it is *intentional,* then you *want* to step on my foot and you *know* my foot is there (and of course you *know how* to step). If one of these is missing, it is an accident.

More generally, a complete intentional action involves motivation, cognition, competence, a physical act, and an outcome or result, as seen in Figure 2.

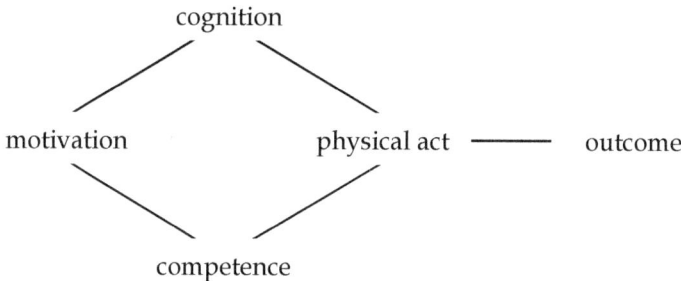

Figure 2: Components of intentional Action

Familiar terms for these components are below

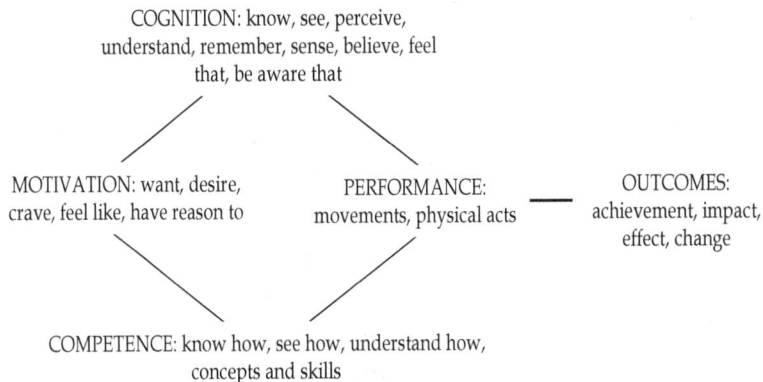

COGNITION: know, see, perceive,
understand, remember, sense, believe, feel
that, be aware that

MOTIVATION: want, desire,
crave, feel like, have reason to

PERFORMANCE:
movements, physical acts

OUTCOMES:
achievement, impact,
effect, change

COMPETENCE: know how, see how, understand how,
concepts and skills

Figure 3: Familiar terms for aspects of successful actions.

A schematic such as this diagrams something which we use implicitly in our everyday observations. It is thus similar to a diagram of a sentence, for it portrays the qualities that those sorts of things must have and do have.

Incomplete acts.

The complete concept makes other, less complete forms of behaviors understandable. An *inadvertent* act or an *accident,* as we have seen, is an act causing an outcome in which one is not trying to cause that outcome. An *attempt* or *try,* on the other hand, is an act done in order to attain an outcome. An *mistake* or *failure* is an unsuccessful attempt, with the outcome not attained.

Note that cognition (seeing and understanding) is included as an integral aspect of behavior. Human action is not a matter of going through life blindly with your eyes closed stumbling into things, but rather a acting on what you see and take to be the case. So while we can observe and consider without acting, we cannot act in a situation without some sense of the situation itself.

Since cognition is an integral aspect of behavior, perceptual, cognitive and mental events are then aspects of behavior. Mental acts are similar to behavior but overt movements and external outcomes are missing. To *see* or to *think* affects what we know about a situation without affecting the situation itself.

Incomplete, dysfunctional, and maladaptive actions are similar but with something amiss. These are characterized by conflicting or maladaptive motivations, by misunderstandings of situations, by misunderstandings of how to promote change, by ineffectual or inappropriate actions, and by failures, losses, and other unwanted outcomes and the accompanying frustrations and misery.

See below:

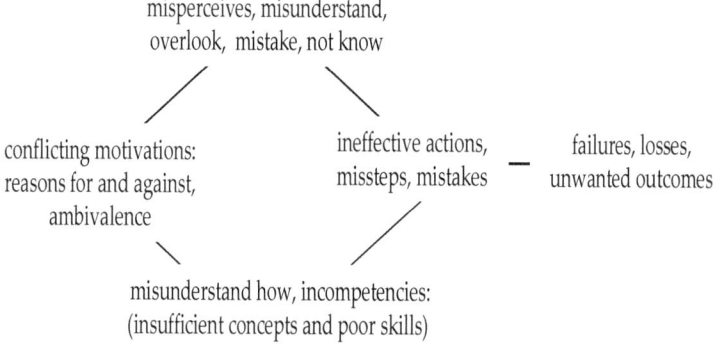

Figure 4: Incomplete or maladaptive actions

The behavior of troubled persons is characteristically incomplete and maladaptive, involving as it often does conflicting motives, misunderstandings, incompetencies, and ill conceived approaches resulting in unsatisfying outcomes. Any of these can be critical in assessment and intervention. Some interventions aim at cognition, some at motivations, some at competencies, and others at outcomes, as is most appropriate to the case at hand.

Organizing theoretical concepts

The schematic also helps us understand concepts from various schools of therapy.

"A behaviorist is someone who pulls habits out of a rat." Anonymous

Behavior: An "operant' is that which has an effect on the environment, and early behaviorists attempted to classify action in general by its measurable impact. "Games" in transactional analysis refer to the ruses or underhanded actions with camouflaged objectives, and "payoffs" then are the achievement of our concealed objectives.

Motivation: Classic psychoanalysis and behaviorism both considered tension reduction and the maintenance of "homeostasis" to be primary motivations, while "actualization" and "growth" are primary in humanistic formulations. Attention is the presumed motivation of behavior therapists, while quest for superiority is primary for Adlerians. Cognitive therapies focus on cognition, of course, but ignore motivational factors almost entirely.

Cognition: Cognition was banished by classical behaviorists, who considered it too mentalistic, bequeathing to later cognitive behaviorists the unaesthetic task of rehabilitating cognition and pasting it into a system designed specifically to eliminate it. "Internal mediating events" were concocted as a odd way to refer to thoughts and feelings and such, which we now refer to by their everyday terms. "Projections," "rationalizations," "transferences," and such from the analytic school refer to misunderstanding.

Competence: A "behavioral repertoire" refers to what one knows how to do, and is thus a competency. Cognitive therapies are strongly interested in the presumptions, confused concepts and unrealistic standards by which we arrive at our misunderstandings.

Performance: These are the "measurables" positivists are so fond of, although note that some actions, such as waiting, have no specific movements at all.

Achievements: "Reinforcers" are officially "stimuli which maintain or increase the frequencies of the preceding behaviors," although the term is commonly used to indicate satisfying outcomes. "Primary reinforcers" are usually physiological necessities, and "secondary reinforcers" are then social or symbolic gains such as attention or money. "Positive reinforcers" are actual gains, and "negative reinforcers" are the resolution of aversive situations. "Overt reinforcers" are observable achievements, whereas "covert" or "self-reinforcers" translate as satisfactions. "Primary gains" in analytic parlance involve tension reduction, and "secondary gains" are social benefits such as the avoidance of responsibility.

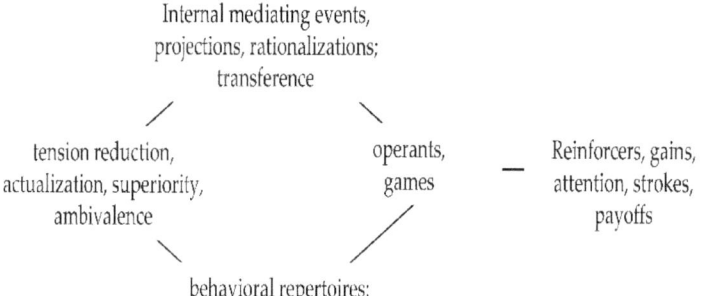

Many of our early theoretical terms continue in our therapy conversations and in our everyday vocabulary, but without the stifling theoretical underpinnings.

Significance

Mom asks "Why," not as a simple question but as some thing more. Mom asks 'Why" as a way to chide and scold her daughter while at the same time camouflaging her accusation. So mom is both asking a question, and scolding . The question is the *way* or *means* by which it is done, and the camouflaged accusation is the *significance* or the *meaning* of the act. Thus, an act can be a means of doing something more, and the something more is the significance of that action.

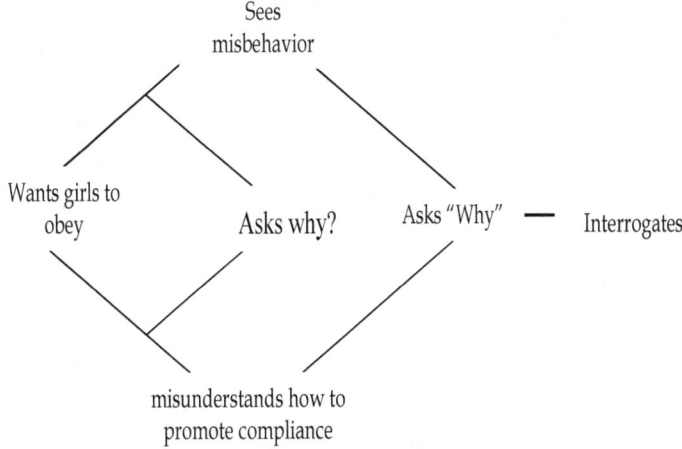

Take it a step or two further. What is mom trying to do by her accusation? A scolding such as we see here might be to punish and thereby promote compliance, or to punish and there extract vengeance and get even . Of course, it might be both.

Suppose mom scolds as a way to hold Brittany accountable for her misbehavior and to force compliance. Here the accusation is the means, and the aim is to correct the misbehavior.

So far as mom is trying to promote compliance, most of us would judge it to a misguided attempt, and we would expect unintended outcomes and further problems. Mom appears to misunderstand how to promote compliance, and Brittany is apt to see the accusation as unfair harsh, and rebel further rather than comply. We would talk to mom about why she is not getting a good outcome and we would introduce better methods to promote compliance.

Scolding also makes sense as an expression of hostility. Suppose mom takes it all personally and feels deeply wronged, and the harshness of her accusation makes it appear clearly hostile. Thus her accusation is payback for the perceived insult.

So far as hostility is a primary motivation, intervention is more difficult. We might try to present a softer account of why a teenage girl might stay out late, to reduce the anger, or talk to mom about how she and Brittany are triggering angry responses from each other and so nudge her toward ways to break the cycle. Obviously, in working with mom, we would have to be careful to avoid the appearance of condoning the misbehavior or of siding against mom or of accusing mom of being overly vindictive.

Skillful clinicians operate at the level of significance, seeing not just what our clients do and say but also what they mean to accomplish by their actions.

Consciousness of actions

Does mom know what she is doing? Well, not necessarily.

You can know how to do something without knowing exactly what you are doing. A cat need not know much about the mechanisms in claws, to know how to use its claws to grasp its prey. You need not know anything about how your eyes processes letters to read the words and understand their meaning. Similarly, mom need not know much about the mechanisms of manipulation to know how to manipulate and to do it quite well.

Similarly, doing something on purpose does not mean that you are necessarily aware of your purpose. The intentional action specified here does not imply that you must be conscious of your intentions. The term "intentional" in ordinary language is used to indicate simple "in order to" action, but also to indicate actions in which you are consciously aware of your aims. Our use of the term here specifies the simpler meaning and specifically excludes the latter reference. Thus, we try to avoid problems of multiple meanings so that key terms may be used in unambiguous ways.

Some actions are something more than simple intentional actions. *Conscious* actions are intentional actions in which the person is aware of her aims and objectives and able to state them.35 *Planned* or *premeditated* actions are intentional actions that are considered ahead of time. Intentional actions contrast with inadvertent acts; conscious actions contrast with unconscious intentional actions; and planned actions contrast with spontaneous or impulsive actions.

Reasons

Intentional action is done in order to accomplish something and thus for some reason. *Reasons* are considerations for actions. Reasons involve both cognition and motivation. More specifically, reasons involve our understanding of things which matter enough to motivate us to act. One who sees herself as neglected has reason to seek attention or companionship; one who sees herself as mistreated or persecuted has reason to seek redress. The observations you make concerning those things that matter to give you reasons to act in particular ways.

The concept is further specified by two simple axioms36 which connect reasons directly to actions. *If a person has a reason to do something he will do it, unless he has a stronger reason not to.* Reasons are seen therefore in the occurrence of behavior, for a person does something when he has sufficient reasons for doing it. And reasons are also seen in the absence of expected behavior, for one does not do something if he sees no reason to do it or if he has a better reason not to. Reasons are reflected in what you say but most clearly in what you do, following the adage that actions speak louder than words. One might have reasons for, and at the same time reasons against doing something, and that corresponds, of course, to conflicts and ambivalence.

Reasons combine together: If a person has a second reason for doing something, then he has a stronger reason than if he had only one of those reasons. Combinations of reasons are involved in many actions, so it is not a matter of one or another of the possible reasons but of whatever combinations of reasons the person actually has. By understanding a combination of several pertinent reasons, we may gain a better analysis of behaviors than we would by committing ourselves to only one of those reasons. "Multiple determination" from psychoanalysis parallels this commonsense view that several reasons for and against may be involved in a particular action.

So mom has reasons for wanting to retaliate against Brittney, who has hurt her, but also reasons for wanting to promote compliance, to raise her properly and have a socially acceptable child. Seeing combinations of reasons gives us additional options on how to intervene.

Note the close connections between perceptions of the world and reasons for action. Seeing Brittany as insulting her gives mom reason to retaliate, whereas seeing the girl as simply failing to comply gives her reason to correct her misbehavior.

Categories of reasons: While any number of reasons are possible, Ossorio observes that human concerns over the centuries can be placed into a few broad categories, and that we can understand ourselves better by seeing which sorts of categories we act upon and which we overlook.

Reasons can be categorized as:

hedonic: pleasure, fun (feels good, smells good, tastes good).

prudential: safety, caution,

moral: right, wrong, fair and unfair

fittingness, which includes beauty, or standard aesthetics, in which components fit together in a way that is pleasing, truth, recognized by whether something fits properly with whatever else is known and social conventions, appropriateness, propriety, and fit with social expectations or individual identity

So while one individual may be so concerned with having enough money for retirement that he works all the time and never enjoys himself, another person may be having such a good that he fails to provide for himself and his future. The first person is prudent, but is missing out on the pleasures of life, while the other person seeks pleasure but overlooks the consequences.

Psychological theories ordinarily focus on one or two of these categories and ignore the others. In its dealings with reinforcers and punishments, for instance, classical behaviorism grapples with pleasure and pain, while overlooking moral reasoning and aesthetic concerns.

Language

The things we say involves the same components as other sorts of action. One says something not merely because it is so or because one thinks, feels, or sincerely believes that it is so. One says things as a way to do something, of responding to a situation, of forwarding an agenda. The words one uses are the means by which it is done, and the reasons and impact comprise the significance of the action.

So here, mom accuses Brittany of wanting to hurt her, as a way to shame Brittany and not so much because she has considered anything carefully and concluded that Brittany must want to hurt her. Yet as she argues her case, she becomes familiar with it until she might be reasonably said to actually believe it.

Activities and Meaning

Much of what is done involves not merely single acts but patterns and sequences of actions, by one or more persons. The issues of significance seen in single acts are similarly important in any activities. One may engage in an activity as a means to further aims or for the satisfactions of the activity itself, with nothing further in mind. One may play soccer as a means of avoiding schoolwork, to practice for an upcoming state championship, to hang with friends, or for the enjoyment of the game (or for some combination of these).

Some activities are ordinarily meaningful in themselves. Raising your children is an obvious instance, in that ordinarily we raise our children because we feel our children are important rather than out of further or ulterior considerations.

Several "in order to" steps may be required to get to the final significance of an activity. A parent may require a child to do his schoolwork in order to encourage him to learn the material, in order to help him attain a good education, in order to provide him with what he needs to do well in life. But such sequences are not endless, and explanation must end somewhere. We arrive sooner or later at something which is being done for its own sake, for the meaning and satisfaction of the social practice itself and not for some further objectives. Full participation in what life might offer includes not just the activities but also the meaning and satisfaction.

Summary

Thus the range of recognizable human behaviors can be easily understood as intentional actions, as incomplete or dysfunctional forms of such actions, as intentional actions with something added, and as combinations and sequences of action. Our conceptualization covers what is considered behavior in everyday conversation, and it also helps to organize the concepts from various theoretical systems.

3 Explanations of Behavior

Why do we act as we do? Look here at what counts as satisfactory explanation.

As simple as it seems, one category of answers involves merely identifying further facets of the behavior itself. One acts because one sees reason to do so and in order to get something one wants.

Why did Brittany stay out late? Perhaps to hang with her boyfriend. Why did mom ask "Why do you want to hurt me?" Perhaps to accuse Brittany, in a concealed manner, to punish her for breaking the rules. In everyday conversation, as a way to explain otherwise puzzling actions we often mention reasons.

We might mention other facets of action as well. We might say a young woman is being cold and aloof toward her fiancé because she sees him as neglectful or untrustworthy. Again, the additional information serves as explanation because it offers a better understanding of previously puzzling actions. Seeing the fiancé as untrustworthy suggest reasons for her actions: Given her opinion of him, she may act aloof to protect herself from a hurtful involvement, to chide him for not taking her concerns seriously, to show him that she expects better.

As our skills improve we become better at seeing facets of actions, and we deal with these with our clients. We see not just the ways our clients act but also their understandings of their situations and the reasons for their actions. More generally, we see not merely the ways clients go about things but also the meaning and significance of what they do.

Situations and Individual Characteristics

Look now at a second order of explanations. Do we attribute the action to the situation, or to qualities of the particular individual. Would most of us in that situation have

have acted about that way? Or does the action indicate specific unique qualities which set an individual apart from the norm?

Why did Brittany stay out past curfew? We might note that her boyfriend got off late and wanted to see her, which explains something. Yet not every girl would stay out just because a boyfriend asked her to. Some comply with curfews while others do not. If she simply lost lost track of time we could and consider her irresponsible, whereas if she knew she would be late we would see her as non-compliant.

What can we say about mom? Many parents impose curfews, so nothing is unusual about that, and most parents react and fuss at youngsters who violate their curfews. It is the way mom fusses which invites a special explanation. Mom seems to take it personally, more than most parents would, and seems especially harsh in her accusations against her daughter. The incident thus suggests that mom tends to take offenses personally, and further, that she tends to be harsher and more punitive than most parents would be in that situation. Were it unusual for her to react so strongly, we would say she was having a bad day. If this sort of reaction is typical, than it is an aspect of her personality. We might also figure that mom has poor conflict resolution skills or, if she has such skills, that she is too offended and angry to put them to use.

As a second illustration consider a man who is jealous of his wife, suspicious that she is having affairs, obsessed, emotionally tormented, and angry. He questions her when she is late or when she is not where she said she would be, and he accuses her continually of being unfaithful. How does one explain the patterns? Does the man have a jealous personality, or is he caught in a tough situation.

Suppose that her actions are reasonable ones and indicate little or no grounds for suspicion, but he treats every minor incident as proof of major wrongdoing, interrogates rashly, and discredits or ignores the answers he is given. Here, the jealousy must be accounted for by the individual characteristics. Others in a similar situation would not act that way.

Suppose on the other hand that the wife frequently comes in late or stays out all night, gives the bewildered fellow little account of her whereabouts, takes calls from unidentified callers, refuses to answer his questions, and complains that he is a suspicious fool and should take care of his own business instead of hers. Here the situation itself provides a sufficient account of the jealousy. Indeed, it would be odd and beg for an explanation if he were not suspicious.

Separating situational and individual personality contributions is essential in assessment and intervention. The jealous husband would have problems either way. But he would not have the same problems. Therapeutic intervention addresses the pertinent contributing factors.

Thus, we account for actions by some combination of situations and individual characteristics. Your "situation" or "circumstances" includes all those aspects of the real world which pertain or might pertain. It includes the opportunities and limitations the situation affords. It includes your relationships, along with the accompanying expectations, pressures, and such, and it includes the status or social position conferred on you by those relationships. Having many friends makes you popular, having a husband makes you a wife, children make you a parent, and so on. Having a job makes you employed as surely as losing a job leaves you unemployed.

Your "individual" qualities or characteristics include the range of inclinations and attitudes and abilities, often collectively referred to as personality, and also the intellectual qualities, that distinguish one individual from another in similar situations.

Thus, Behavior is understandable from Situations and Individual Differences.

Entire behavioral sequences of observation, emotion, motivation, performance and outcome are understandable from situational and individual factors. What the jealous husband sees is understandable from his wife's actions and from his inclinations; what he feels is understandable from what he sees and from his standards and attitudes toward such things; what he does is understandable from his observations, from his feelings and motivations, and from the available opportunities.

Situations

Several concepts from familiar theories refer to aspects of situations. The term "stimuli" was introduced to signify a physically measurable aspects of a situation, while "environment" refer to any aspect of a situation. "Antecedents" are events which evoke an action.

General adversities are "unconditioned aversive stimuli" in behaviorism and "activating events" in the rational emotive ABC formulation. "Discriminative stimuli in operant conditioning signify whether or not an opportunity exists .Various concepts and terms from familiar theoretical formulations are thus identifiable as facets of situations.

Individual Characteristics

Individual characteristics are distinctive inclinations and abilities to see, to evaluate, and to act in particular ways; these include the range of intellectual and personality characteristics. Individual characteristics concepts refer to inclinations and abilities, and are not implicit or overt references to physiological structures and processes.

One's concepts are the distinctions one uses to observe and structure his world. "Constructs" from personal construct theory refer to the individual's concepts. An individual retains information and misinformation which he can recall and apply; intelligence is the ability to figure things out.

One's standards and related beliefs are value-laden distinctions, and correspond to the ways one sees and evaluates things on a good/bad dimension. Persons have standards of right and wrong, and beliefs that some things are right and good while other things are wrong and awful. The evaluations one makes serve as the most reliable indication of his standards and beliefs.

Similar concepts are included in several orientations. "Belief systems" in Ellis's ABC rational-emotive formulation are used to evaluate adversities: someone with "rational beliefs" evaluates adversities as tolerable and manageable; someone with "irrational beliefs" sees them as intolerable and catastrophic. "Personal injunctions" in transactional analysis are beliefs that particular actions are not permitted and should not be done. Self-concept problems in client-centered formulations usually involve harsh personal standards by which one evaluates oneself as wrong and bad. In behaviorism, "conditioned aversive stimuli" are conditions which a particular individual sees as threatening and stressful: direct references to standards and beliefs are omitted, but the issues are covered nonetheless by these supposedly more objective equivalents. From separate orientations, these concepts cover similar tendencies to evaluate things as intolerable, not permissible, unacceptable, aversive, or otherwise unpleasant and wrong.

Traits are tendencies to act in particular ways across situations. "Probabilities" and "frequencies" refer to the same things for the behaviorist: where we would ordinarily say a child tends to be disruptive or simply is disruptive, a behaviorist covers the same ground by saying that he emits a high frequency of disruptive behaviors. Tendencies to involve oneself in particular patterns are termed "scripts" in transactional analysis.

Values and interests are what matters. These are one's priorities-what one would be motivated to accomplish, everything else being equal. Among its many meanings, the term "reinforcer" in behaviorism refers to that which an individual values and is interested in striving to achieve.

Competencies include one's concepts, memory, and intelligence, which are cognitive abilities, and also skills, which are performance abilities. "Behavioral repertoires" in behaviorism correspond to skills-what one is competent to do. These factors appear directly as the "know-how" aspect of behavior.

States are fluctuations in individual tendencies: in a particular state, a person tends to respond somewhat differently from the ways in which he would respond if not in that state. While angry or exhausted, one has tendencies that one does not have when calm or rested. States might involve emotions (angry, afraid), moods (excited), attitudes (intrigued), or energy level (alert, exhausted). The "hours of food deprivation" parameter in operant conditioning indicates a state of hunger in which the animal is motivated to strive for food. "Parent, adult, and child (P-A-C)" ego states in transactional analysis indicate fluctuating tendencies to act in ways loosely similar to parents, adults, and children. The critical parent state indicates a critical attitude, the nurturing parent state, a supportive attitude; the adult state, thoughtfulness; the free child state is a playful mood, and the adapted child state is a compliant or rebellious stance toward authority. Transactional analysis is wedded to categorizing actions by their origins in one or another of these ego states.

In this manner, concepts from various theories are easily organized and blended into our ordinary language concepts.

Behavior is understood from situations and individual characteristics; thus, the behavioral explanation formula $B = f(S \& IC)$. The three factors are conceptually related, in that any two of them can be used to estimate the third —as in geometry when two angles of a triangle are given, the third can be calculated. Each factor is logically understandable from the other two: behavior from situations and individual characteristics; individual characteristics from behavior, with allowances made for the situations; and situations themselves from the persons' reaction, with allowances made for distinctive individual characteristics.

Situations, Circumstances
relationships, status,
opportunities, limitations,
stimuli, antecedents,
environments

Behavior

Individual Characteristics,
traits, attitudes, interests,
abilities, knowledge, values,
states, powers,
personality & intelligence,

The complementary categories of situations and individual characteristics include all present psychological factors which contribute to behavior, for the rule here is that anything that does contribute must be placed in one or the other of these two categories. The formula is thus tautological, and it is this obvious and non-falsifiable quality which makes it suitable as a conceptual tool to structure empirical observations.

Specific behaviors, situations, and individual characteristics go together in ways that should make sense. In our everyday perceptions, we rely on configurations of these three factors to see what is going on. Observations of any two of the factors provide a cross-check for our observation or estimate of the third because, if they do not go together properly, then an error has been made in one or more of the observations. We may use estimates of any two of the factors to evaluate and improve our estimates of the third. The logical relatedness of these factors is especially important in clinical practice, where we must make observations and estimates based on sometimes less than adequate information. We can cross-check our observations against other observations and see if things add up properly.

The use of situations and individual characteristics to understand behavior is a commonsense idea, and is adapted into several familiar formulations. In Lewin's field theory, behavior is a function of the person and the environment. In S-O-R behavior theory, the Stimulus acts through the Organism to elicit a Response. In Ellis's rational emotive ABC formulation, Activating events are interpreted by Belief systems to yield emotional Consequences. S-O-R behaviorism weights the situation, which acts through the individual to yield behavior, while the rational-emotive formulation weights the beliefs of the individual, which interpret the situation. Each formula has its own unique qualities, but the everyday concept of behavior as understandable from situational and individual characteristics runs through all of them.

The familiar orientations can be classified and rated on their management of each of these three factors. Analytic orientations tend to overlook situational contributions, while family systems formulations in contrast are strong on relationship and social position factors but tend to ignore individual personality characteristics. The reputation which behaviorists have for ignoring individual personality factors is unwarranted, since individual differences factors are camouflaged but included nonetheless in the behaviorists' own unique concepts and terms.

Persons

Persons are extremely complex beings, and a rich variety of concepts is available to characterize what may be interesting and important about particular persons. The concepts used in ordinary language and also in psychological and social sciences to characterize persons can be seen to fall easily into the three categories of behavioral, social situational, and individual personality characteristics outlined here. Persons engage in patterns of actions, and are identified and characterized by what they see and do in their lives and, thus, by their behavioral characteristics. Persons live and act in networks of social relationships, and are characterized by their noteworthy status or positions in these social relationships and, thus, by their situational characteristics. Persons also have distinctive individual inclinations and abilities, and are characterized by their noteworthy intellectual and personality characteristics.

For instance, we could describe Joanie Caucus as one who spends her days settling squabbles (behaviors), as one who has a job as a day-care mother (status and social position), and as one who values teaching children to treat each other fairly (individual characteristics). Each of these says something about Joanie and identifies her as who she is. Similarly, we could describe the jealous husband as one who interrogates his wife continually (behaviors), as the husband of a longsuffering but quite faithful woman (status and marital situation), and as one who has a suspicious bent (individual characteristics).

Through descriptions from one or more of these three categories, we identify and communicate what is noteworthy about particular persons. Persons are also identified by their physical appearances; therefore, physical characteristics are included as a fourth attribute of persons.

Acquisition of present features.

Our third order of explanation involves the ways by which present situations and individual characteristics were acquired. How did the circumstances and relationships in which the person is involved come about, and how did he acquire the particular individual characteristics that he has? How, in other words, did he get to be where he is, and how did he get to be who he is? We look to past occurrences to answer these questions.

Social Transitions

Major changes in one's circumstances, relationships, and status are commonly referred to as transitions. Such transitions include any form of social inclusion, promotion, accreditation, and gain, or social exclusion, demotion, degradation, and loss. Familiar examples of social transitions are leaving home, graduating, finding a job or losing one, making friends or enemies, gaining recognition or losing favor, breaking up with a sweetheart, getting married, becoming a parent, retiring, and so on. Such changes may be instigated by one's own actions, but they also involve the attitudes and actions of other persons.

If the wife were indeed unfaithful, as the husband so strongly suspects, then we might ask how he became involved in that sort of marriage. Perhaps as a youngster he was introverted and inexperienced. A young girl wanted to get away from home and grabbed on to him with all the affection one might have for a "get out of jail free" card. He,

in his insecurity and naiveté, missed the obvious expediency and had barely adjusted to marriage by the time she had her sights set on greener pastures. (To hear his mother, it would seem that all mothers' sons are lost to marriage in just this manner. Consider this nonetheless as merely one of many possibilities.)

On the other hand, perhaps they were well suited for each other in their early relationship, but he was committed to his work and insensitive to her concerns and feelings, and would not involve himself in the intimacies which should be expected in a marriage. He ignored or misunderstood her attempts to talk about the problem, and out of loneliness and boredom, she turned to another man. Thus he finds himself very much on the outside.

Perhaps he was committed to a liberal ideology that opposes the restrictiveness and lack of freedom of marriage. He argued his wife into it, and together they embarked on an open marriage in which each of them would be allowed to have intimacies with others outside of the marriage. It sounded free and exciting in principle, but now that it is really

34

happening things are frighteningly out of control. The husband has feelings that he had not expected and finds the situation intolerable.

Any number of other explanations are also possible, of course, for there are countless ways one gets involved in particular situations: the actual explanations must be based on observation and analysis of the case at hand. These explanations are essentially social histories which should take into account the sequences of behavioral, situational, and individual factors by which the situation came about. The explanation of how this man got involved with an unfaithful wife might say something about the choices he makes, about his incompatibilities with this particular woman, or perhaps about the problems of choosing a mate early in life and on the basis of necessarily limited information. An explanation of how current relationships were acquired might be used to better understand the natures of the persons involved. Problem situations are the offspring of limited vision and maladaptive inclinations, of the inconsiderateness or ill will of others, and also of unfortunate and sometimes unavoidable happenstance.

Some orientations suggest more general explanations. Analytic and related orientations focus on the needs being fulfilled through messy relationships, implying that the person has unconscious motivations to be involved in such problems. Transactional analysis emphasizes "scripts," which are plans for one's life, and holds that messy situations occur because one follows a script to bring them about. Social transitions are dealt with at considerable length in sociology and anthropology, and to lesser extent, in social psychology and in relationship and family approaches to psychotherapy.

Learning and Maturation
individual characteristics are acquired through learning and through a broad wastebasket category which includes maturation and "other than learning" factors.

Were the wife faithful but the husband characteristically jealous, then we might ask how he acquired that individual

35

personality characteristic. Perhaps in a first marriage he was secure and settled but his wife was not, and she played the field continually for the duration of their marriage. Unable to forgive or forget, he became embittered toward women and hardened himself against ever caring enough to be vulnerable. So he carries his hurt and rage over to his present wife and now looks for betrayal.

On the other hand, perhaps as a youngster his mother showered him with attention and special considerations but was cold and embittered toward his father, so that he came to see affection from a woman as something given to a child but not to a man. These views render him unable as a man to accept love and nurturance from a woman, for a woman's love makes him feel small and dependent. In the marriage, he has expected his wife to be weaker and to look up to him, which has not always been possible since she is herself a competent and successful person and he, because of human limitations, is not always a hero. He has thus been unable to accept the love and reassurance which she gives, and unable also to gain reassurance through his ideal of masculine superiority. He has become easily annoyed at his wife, feeling she does not respect and love him, and his annoyance has made matters worse, for the marriage suffers by comparison to his wife's outside friendships. In this manner he has become increasingly insecure, suspicious, and jealous, trapped not by his wife but by his own misconceptions.

Perhaps he became infatuated with his secretary, and has felt guilty about it and troubled that his wife might find out. If his wife were also interested in somebody else, then that would be equitable and would

allay his guilt; he fantasizes that she might be interested, and finds himself both intrigued and aroused by the thought, but also insecure and angry that she would do such a thing. The imaginings come to seem too real; he becomes unreasonably suspicious of his wife and accuses her of wanting other men.

There are any number of ways one can become overly suspicious, and jealous, just as there are any number of ways one can acquire any of a range of other distinctive individual characteristics. If someone has a given personality characteristic, he has acquired it in one of the ways in which it can be acquired, but not necessarily in the same way it might have been acquired by someone else. We are cautioned, therefore, against expecting any single generalization or theory to provide a reliable account of how individual characteristics are acquired. We must observe and investigate, for adequate understanding is based on adequate observation of the particular case at hand.

In clinical practice the issue is not so much how the person acquired a particular characteristic, but rather how he can alter or rearrange troublesome tendencies and acquire more constructive ones. The means by which present characteristics were acquired maybe of some importance nonetheless, for they may give some leads to the means by which current changes may be made and more beneficial characteristics acquired. Learning occurs through what one sees and does, and is thus an outcome of one's behaviors. One learns new inclinations and abilities through observations and practice. The category of learning includes insight and conditioning, training and socialization, learning through observation and learning by participation, study (intended learning) and unplanned everyday learning, and so on.

Some generalizations of how learning occurs are included in most major theories of behavior, personality, psychopathology and psychotherapy. Behavioral orientations emphasize "conditioning," which refers (as in ordinary language) to learning that occurs through continuing and often wearisome repetitions. In operant conditioning, "reinforcement"-the achievement of something one wants-is a quite obvious way of learning which acts get you what you want. "Extinction"-the failure to gain what you want-is a way of learning which acts are ineffective. The term "modeling" refers to teaching by example.

Several formulations see adversities as the means by which one learns troublesome tendencies. In behavioral orientations, fears of things are learned from repeated pairings of those things with other things which are themselves naturally frightening. Being subject to "parental injunctions" in transactional analysis leads youngsters to acquire their own restrictive personal injunctions, from which they construct scripts. In client-centered formulations, the "conditions of worth" by which one is judged lead youngsters to judge aspects of themselves as wrong and unacceptable, to deny those aspects, and by so doing to invite further problems.

Several orientations-notably analytic, dynamic, and object-relations-suggest that the early years are of more importance in acquiring personality characteristics, while others, most notably behavioral orientations, emphasize that learning continues to change individual characteristics throughout life. An excellent review of the research by Kagan et al. (1978) suggests that the importance of infancy and early childhood has been overestimated, and that later childhood and adolescent experiences are more important in personality development. Some suggest that the young adult years may be the most important. In any case, we do not have to focus on any single age but should keep our eyes open to influences which occur at whatever ages.

Maturation Individual characteristics are acquired by processes other than learning, notably by maturation, by changes generally explained physiologically, and also by transient state changes. Maturation includes increases in intellectual abilities and personal maturity as one grows up, sexual maturation, and so on. Those changes attributable directly to physiological factors include changes in temperament from poor nutrition, senility, or other types of brain impairment, and any of the range of changes caused by the actions of various psychotropic medications. Examples of state changes include becoming confused from too little sleep or becoming immobilized by fear. While some of these changes are explained by physiological factors, it is the changes themselves, and not the physiological explanations, which belong in our present categorization of psychological explanations.

The various explanations here are obviously quite diverse, for the only real requirement for placing intellectual and personality changes in this "other than learning" wastebasket is that they cannot be attributed to learning.

The Structure of Psychological Explanation

Thus, the three orders of explanations are:

1. Additional aspects of the action itself which help one to understand other aspects of the action that appear puzzling

2. Some combination of situations and/or individual characteristics which explain why someone does something.

3. The means by which such situations and/or individual characteristics were acquired

Together these should cover the range of what are used as everyday psychological explanations and the range also of behavioral and social sciences explanations.

The categorization scheme is outlined in Figure 9. Behavior is thus explained by situations and individual characteristics, which in turn are explained by how they were acquired. The outline includes present factors (behavior, situations, and individual characteristics) and past factors (social transitions, and learning and maturation). The outline is not itself an explanation for behavior, but rather a way of organizing the various sorts of explanations. The scheme has been constructed to cover the entire range of what qualifies as psychological explanation. Answers to the question, Why did he do that? are given through descriptions of factors in one or more of these categories.

Plausible explanations from each category can be collected together in a single illustration. Suppose a young woman said "No!," and we wish to explain why. It is a simple enough behavior, involving as it does only one word, and only one syllable at that. But no behavior is necessarily that simple, and this one should do for an illustration. Look first to the behavior itself: Perhaps she said no because she misunderstood the man's intentions, in order to get out of a commitment, or in order to pay him back in spades for making her so insecure. Look next to the situation or individual characteristics which make the behavior understandable: she said no to his invitation because he called so late in the week or because he had been showing interest in another girl; and she said no because she is used to having her own way all the time and has a spiteful streak when someone crosses her. Look finally to the way the situation and individual characteristics were acquired: she was in this mess with him because she had been cold and aloof, and had taken him for granted; and she is tempermental because she was ignored while growing up, but she could get what she wanted by throwing a scene and was never taught to compromise. We get a good explanation here of the whys of the woman's behavior.

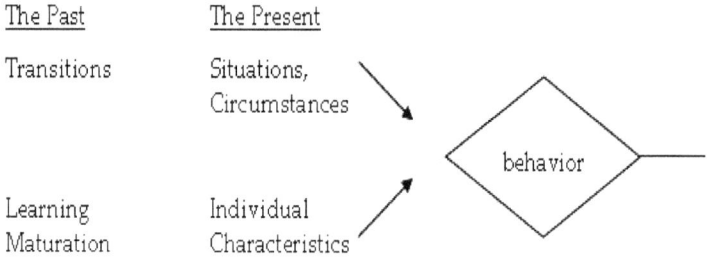

Figure 9.Explanations of behavior.

The scheme categorizes everyday psychological explanations as well as behavioral and social sciences explanations. Several key concepts from familiar theoretical formulations have been shown to fit easily into our common language categories, and other concepts could be shown to fit in much the same manner. Some of these concepts are roughly equivalent to ordinary language concepts and can be easily translated into ordinary language. Other concepts are not directly translatable, but can be better understood and organized by the common language system. The categorization system is argued to be complete not because every conceivable explanation has been shown to fit, but rather on the basis of logical considerations. All psychological explanations of behavior fit logically into one or more of these broad categories.

These are explanations of behavior, and some qualify also as causes. In everyday conversation, people speak about what causes you to feel or act the way you do, or the cause of your problems, but causes and causal language must be understood as shorthand. Every behavioral event is understandable from several contributing factors, and each of those factors is understandable in turn from numerous other contributing factors. Thus, things are understandable from configurations and sequences of contributing factors. But not all such contributing factors can be noted, and mentioning one or two of them usually provides enough information to suit your purposes. What people refer to as "causes" then are contributing factors which have particular relevance to their purposes. See "cause" as shorthand for "noteworthy contributing factor."

The various psychological theories deal with particular aspects from one or more of these explanatory categories and frequently broaden them into purportedly general explanations of human behavior. These theories can be compared and contrasted on the basis of which aspects they focus on and which they ignore.

There are domains of explanation outside the strictly psychological explanations outlined here, including physiological explanations and, in obvious contrast, theological and mystical explanations. Physiological explanations, such as androgens, endorphins, seratonin levels and such, are descriptions of physiological entities and processes. Spiritual explanations, such as God's will or a plan for our lives, a guardian angel or guide or a deamon, and such, are portrayals of a higher order or meaning of life or of agents in another realm. Physiological explanations enjoy a widespread respectability, while theological and mystical explanations are often considered speculative and unconfirmable. The strictly psychological concepts outlined here do not compete with physiological or other explanations of human actions, but are expected to complement and coordinate with them.

This system of concepts has a breadth and completeness which qualifies it as a single system through which we might try to understand the range of concerns in the behavioral and social sciences. It thus meets the initial requirements for a comprehensive eclectic framework. We might need further observations and better analysis to explain something, and we might need more effective interventions. What we do not need is to try to abandon the structure of our familiar, ordinary language concepts and to replace them with something else.

4
Psychological Problems and Psychotherapy

Our concepts of psychological impairments (psychopathology) and psychotherapy follow from our concept of human action .

Psychological Problems

What is it that is wrong with persons, that is treated through psychotherapy? Everyone has some grasp of the concept of psychological problems–or psychopathology–although it may be difficult to articulate. The various names for such problems include maladjustment, problems in living, instability or emotional instability, mental disorder and-in its more serious form-mental illness or insanity. Theories of psychopathology focus variously on underlying pathogens, on mental or emotional states, on overt behaviors, on families, or on larger social organizations. Analytic and dynamic orientations see the pathology not in overt actions but in underlying inner conflicts which are viewed as causes of the manifest symptoms. Behavioral orientations see pathology in the observable behaviors themselves. Family systems orientations see the pathology not in the individual or in his behavior, but in family relationships which are viewed as the cause of individual symptoms. These are all related to each other in that they are theories of the same thing – psychopathology. An explicit concept of psychopathology is necessary in order to clarify the essential relatedness of these viewpoints.

Disorders are best understood via their relation to proper functioning, and so too with mental disorders. A range of

43

social practices or ways of life is generally available to persons: full participation in a way of life includes the activities and the meaning and satisfaction as well. A healthy person is one who is able to participate and find meaning in available social practices; an unhealthy person, by contrast, is one who is impeded in his ability to do so. Thus, the concept of mental disorder: psychopathology is a significant restriction in one's ability to participate fully in available social practices (cf. Ossorio, 1983).

The concept of restriction in abilities is seen as well with physiologcal or medical illnesses. One might easily imagine two persons having the same strain of virus, with one person feeling ill and restricted to bed rest, and the second person feeling well and continuing normal daily activities; the effects of a virus are not the same for everyone. In the first case the virus is a pathogen-a disease-while in the second case it is merely an innocuous foreign agent. In physiology as in psychology, a condition qualifies as a form of pathology to the extent that it impedes healthy functioning. In psychology we are mainly concerned not with physiological conditions but with behavioral, social, and personality factors which impede healthy participation.

Consider excessive alcohol consumption as a common dysfunctional behavior pattern. One might easily imagine two persons who drink the same amount but who are affected differently by it. One of them misses work and is about to get fired, has little personal involvement with his wife, family, or former friends, and lies to himself and others to cover the extent of his drinking. The second man, in contrast, manages his job well, is personable and conscientious, enjoys family and friends, and jokes good naturedly about his excessive drinking. The first person, all would agree, is an alcoholic, and has disabling mental or emotional problems. The second man, in contrast, should not be considered to have serious mental or emotional problems, in that he is able to participate in his version of what appears to be a meaningful and enjoyable way of life. It is thus the limitations imposed by alcohol, rather than the amount one consumes, which qualify alcohol consumption as a common form of psychopathology.

Similarly, unresolved insecurities and resentments toward one's mother and father may impede one's abilities to manage present relationships with persons in authority, and so qualify as causes of present psychological problems. Similar resentments which do not impede present relationships are of less importance and would not qualify as psychopathology. The same principle applies in family relationships. Dysfunctional families may undermine and confuse, and bring forth the worst in individual family members. To the extent that they so impede healthy participation, families too are rightly seen as causes of psychopathology.

Any factors which restrict participation might qualify as causes of psychopathology. Causes thus might be situational or personality factors, or the experiences and actions which are understandable from, and in turn generate, such problem factors. The past conditions by which such factors were acquired might also be included as causes. The various theories of psychopathology stake out positions on which such factors are most important.

Psychological and emotional problems are understood from situational and individual characteristics in the same way that anything one does is so understood. Situational and individual factors are primary means of understanding and categorizing adjustment problems, and of understanding and organizing intervention techniques which address such problems. These factors are therefore included in our concept of psychopathology. Situations are included because particular situations introduce stresses which overtax existing capabilities and so cause psychological problems. Individual characteristics are included because troubled individuals are often especially weak in their abilities to manage a wide range of situations.

Matches or mismatches between situations and individual characteristics are also important. Individuals have their own unique needs and inclinations which make them well suited to some situations and not to others. One individual may thrive on structure and be confused and miserable without it; another may thrive on independence and be stifled by structure; and the very same two individuals who were so filled with love and optimism living together as singles may be trapped and miserable together as marrieds. We need to weigh both factors, and the matches or mismatches between the factors. Problems arise from stressful situations which overtax otherwise adequate abilities, from general inabilities to manage much of anything at all, and from unfortunate mismatches between one's circumstances and one's individual inclinations or abilities.

Experiences and actions, social relationships, and personality characteristics generally interweave in any adequate case analysis, and should be seen as complementary rather than as competing explanations of psychopathology. It is not experiences versus actions, or social relationships versus personality which is "the cause" of psychopathology. Rather, it is configurations and patterns of these factors which cause psychopathology: We understand the problems as we weigh the contributions of such factors and see the necessary interconnectedness among them.

Present and past contributing factors must be clearly separated. Present contributing factors may be explained by factors in the immediate past, and those explained by factors further in the past, and so on in endless sequence: each present contributing factor has a continuing chain of past factors which contributed to bring it about. Behavior is understood from situations and individual characteristics, and these in turn from the means by which they came about, and these in turn from the means by which they came about, and so on. Present relationships, personality characteristics, and consequent experiences and actions are the immediate causes of psychological problems; past occurrences were the causes then of these present causes.

A person's participation is seen as restricted by comparison to some appropriate, healthy, or even exceptional alternatives. We see inabilities by comparing what the person actually does with what one might do instead which would be more adaptive. In clinical assessment, it is important to understand what might be appropriate or healthy ways of managing existing situations and to see the occurring patterns as indications of an inability to respond in any of those healthy ways.

Awareness of an individual's inabilities also makes existing unconstructive patterns more understandable. When a situation calls for a person to do something he is unable to do, then he will do something he can do. Inappropriate and problematic actions are necessarily indications of an inability to act in a more adaptive and fulfilling manner.

Consider a woman who is taken advantage of, and mistreated by, family and friends, and who by her passivity allows the mistreatment to continue. Such a person might in turn lose confidence in herself and feel she is a worthless nobody, or she might find self-righteous satisfaction in being morally better than those who mistreat her and thus maintain a secret sense of superiority. She might become resentful, undermine and manipulate others to get her way, and so further spoil her social relationships; or she might have explosive outbursts of anger and become afraid that she is losing control of herself. She might hold others responsible for her life and so avoid taking responsibility herself. She might withdraw from close relationships to avoid the anguish they entail. Such patterns are all understandable manifestations of the mistreatment this woman is unable to stand up against. They are all related here, in that they are all manifestations of the same restricted ability to make the necessary stands and so redress the mistreatment. An assessment of this case might include any of the existing behavioral, social, and personality factors. One should surely mention what this woman is unable to do which, if she could do, would solve the existing problems. Most fundamentally, she is unable to make stands, and anything which addresses that inability would improve the surrounding manifestations of the problem.

47

Thus, good clinical analysis looks at what one is doing which contributes to the problems, and at the situational and individual characteristics which make what one is doing understandable. It also looks at what the person might be doing instead which would alleviate the problems, at the situational and individual changes which would enable him to do that, and at the ways in which we might bring those changes about. The objective of therapy then is to bridge the gap to enable the person to do that which would solve the problems.

The same factors which are manifestations of the problem may also be additional contributing factors which further augment the problem. If the mistreatment causes the woman to feel she is a worthless nobody or to construct a secret superiority to those who mistreat her, then these contribute in turn in her continuing passivity and must be addressed in an attempt to promote assertiveness. She becomes assertive as she gains some confidence in herself, sees that she has the right to make stands, and chooses the challenges of confrontations over the familiar safety of resenting those who take advantage of her. When her assertive stands are successful, her rights become established, her social relationships improve, and her confidence in herself increases, thus further altering the original pattern. In turn, these more constructive alternatives make it easier to relinquish the resentments and other satisfactions of the passive victim position and to continue asserting herself.

Mental, emotional and behavioral, and social and personality factors are thus seen as causes, as consequent manifestations, and from there as further causes of restricted abilities to participate. It is through the identification and alleviation of factors which are causes that one alleviates major restrictions in abilities to participate.

Social practices involve sequences and patterns of actions, and an inability to do any of the necessary particulars may thus restrict participation in the entire practice. On a specific level, psychopathology is a restriction in one's ability to engage in those actions necessary to available social practices. Major restrictions in functioning may be due to circumscribed failures and limitations, and in such cases alleviating seemingly minor inabilities may have major constructive benefits to a person's overall well-being. In other cases the problems are broader and more embedded. In the case just described, an inability to be appropriately assertive severely impedes the woman's participation in more satisfying forms of social relationships. Better social relationships and better ways of life become available through the alleviation of such critical inabilities.

The concept of psychopathology involves significant restrictions in abilities. We all have limitations, of course, for everyone has some areas in which he or she is less than adequate and more limited than many others. These various psychological limitations do not thereby qualify as psychopathology, however, in so far as their impact remains manageable. It is only when personal limitations result in a major inability to participate that the condition qualifies as psychopathology.

Clinical cases involve complex and often unique configurations of mental and behavioral, social, and personality patterns. Traditional diagnostic taxonomies are generally considered to be crude and over-inclusive categorizations, and more important, to be oftentimes irrelevant as a basis for psychotherapeutic interventions. Our alternative here is the use of individual case formulations which attempt to grasp the essentials of a particular case so as to provide a basis for therapeutic treatment. The emphasis here is not on any particular theory of psychopathology, but rather on individual case formulations.

Given the vast complexities, how are we to figure out what our clients might do to improve themselves and improve their situations? What is the right course, that we might suggest? Look at the most general standard: Given her personal limitations and the obvious hardships she faces, what would a sensible person do in that situation?[37] So far as we are sensible individuals we can figure out a sensible solution, we can present it and try sell it to our clients, and get them started in the right direction. So far as we are not particularly astute with our own lives, we might still have a chance. Ask not what your yourself would do, but we step outside of yourself and ask what a truly sensible person would do. Perhaps a sensible solution is still within reach.

Psythotherapy

A definition of psychotherapy follows directly from our concept of psychopathology: Psychotherapy is an attempt to alleviate restrictions in one's abilities to participate in meaningful ways of life. The cornerstone of the definition is in the objectives and purpose. One might also mention that psychotherapy involves a relationship between therapist and client, that the client mentions problems and the therapist gives interpretations and suggestions, and so on. Our concept is anchored here by its purpose, and the various particulars follow as the means to that purpose.

Psychotherapy is an attempt to alleviate restrictions, for we intervene in order to accomplish the aims and objectives but there is no guarantee each time that any intervention will be successful. The practice must be anchored by its aims and objectives because, since particular techniques and procedures are not always effective, they are unsuitable therefore as defining attributes.

Psychotherapy is conceived of broadly enough here to include any psychological interventions which are conducted to gain therapeutic changes. It includes methods traditionally considered verbal approaches and those considered behavioral approaches. The requirement is that interventions are done in order to redress limitations in abilities to participate.

The concepts of behavior, situations, and individual characteristics so important in understanding psychopathology are likewise important in its treatment. One who seeks therapy generally does so because she is living a life in which she is dissatisfied and because she is unable on his own to alter it for the better. As ways of life are generated from situations and individual characteristics, so too are changes in ways of life brought about through changes in these factors. Major changes are attained usually through combinations and sequences of changes in behaviors, circumstances, and personality characteristics. Entering psychotherapy, for instance, is itself a change in one's circumstances, for it introduces a new and important relationship, gives one a place or status within that relationship, and subjects one to the various influences of the therapeutic endeavor. The process of psychotherapy changes one's individual characteristics, for one acquires new ways of seeing things and acting which are carried into other areas of his life. Changes in one's actions, in turn, generate further changes in his relationships as others come to see him in new ways and treat him differently. These changes, in turn, improve one's confidence and lead to further changes in one's own attitudes and inclinations, and so the process continues.

A program of assertiveness training to alter passivity might convince the client that he does have rights; challenge the attitudes which contribute to passivity, including his tendency to blame others whenever things go wrong; show how assertive responses can solve his problems; introduce and illustrate appropriate responses, and have the client practice them; and provide social support for his efforts in order to improve his confidence. The immediate objective is to increase his inclinations and abilities to act assertively. The client may be extremely apprehensive during his initial assertive responses, but by acting assertively, he may establish his rights, and improve his status and position in social relationships. In turn, improvements in relationships should improve confidence and outlook, and provide a friendlier atmosphere in which to live. Here, changes in individual characteristics, actions, and social relationships go hand in hand.

Some interventions work by changing attitudes and abilities so that the client more easily adapts to existing circumstances. Others work by changing directly the circumstances the individual faces: an obnoxious youngster might be treated through consultation with his parents to teach them to be stricter and more consistent, so that the youngster faces fewer opportunities to profit by misbehavior and better benefits for cooperation.

In marital and family sessions, there are opportunities to directly affect the attitudes of each individual and the relationships other family members have toward that individual. The opportunity to generate complementary changes in both personality characteristics and relationships is one of the major benefits of marital and family sessions.

Several familiar orientations might be loosely characterized by their attempts to change primarily one or the other of these complementary factors. Those focusing on managing situations and relationships include behavior modification and family systems orientations; those emphasizing individual personality changes include psychoanalytic, psychodynamic, object relations, client-centered, and Gestalt approaches. As eclectics we observe and weigh both situational and personality aspects of client problems, and are free to draw upon insights and techniques from any of the various orientations as we see fit.

The focus here is on changing present factors, and the role of the past should be mentioned. The past is connected logically to situations and individual characteristics since these were acquired through past experiences. However, the constraints the past places on present options are too easily overestimated. Clients sometimes ask: "Since the way I am is caused by my past, and I cannot alter my past, then how can I expect to change?" Note that the question leaves out the important intermediate concept of individual characteristics and goes directly from past learning to current behavior. A good answer involves reintroducing individual characteristics; for example, we might say: "What you have learned from the past are ways of seeing and reacting to things, which are essentially habits. The habits exist not in your past but in your present, and can be changed. Change the habits, and the spell of your past is broken."

Only present contributing factors are subject to change, and therapeutic improvements occur through changes in factors which are in the present entirely and not in the past. We can change someone's memories of past experiences and we can change the significance she gives to those experiences, but the past itself is completed and immutable, and it cannot be changed. The logic of this point need not be taken as a prejudice against talking about the past. We might investigate the past in order to make better sense of existing problems and to help the client restructure his (present) understanding of himself and of his relationships. Investigation of the past is thus a means to understand or try to change present viewpoints, but it is not a logical requirement for therapeutic changes and should not be seen as a necessary objective in and of itself.

Procedural Guidelines

Some aspects of therapeutic interventions are specific to each individual client, and other aspects are more generally important in any therapeutic situation. The specific ways we phrase things are usually adapted to the individual client and to the particulars of the problems, as are the ways we sequence the interventions. But everything need not be figured anew each moment with each individual case. The nature of psychotherapy is such that there are identifiable principles and objectives which are generally important across sessions, and with a wide variety of clients, as the means to attain therapeutic outcomes. These more general aspects of psychotherapy are presented in the following chapters as guidelines for therapeutic practice.

The guidelines are themselves objectives which are steps toward the overall objective of alleviating restricted-abilities.

As-intermediate objectives, they bridge the gap between the overall objectives of therapy and the particular play-by-play interventions by which such objectives

are accomplished (cf. Holmes, 1970). Particular statements are made in order to accomplish these guideline objectives, which in turn are in order to accomplish the more general overall objectives. The guidelines are prescriptive in that they are suggestions to act to attain particular outcomes and to avoid others. The guidelines are the doables and "do not-ables" of therapeutic practice.

Various familiar techniques can be seen as attempts to attain one or more of the guideline objectives, and a variety of apparently unsimilar techniques may be classified together because they are used to attain the same or similar changes. The guidelines serve in this way to organize the use of familiar techniques from separate orientations. The guidelines serve also to help generate and understand new and creative interventions, for they specify the general objectives and give leeway for us to tailor the ways we accomplish those objectives.

Each of the guidelines presented is a synthesis of the practical good sense that runs through one or more, and in some cases a majority, of the various approaches to psychotherapy. Some of the guidelines are easily seen as summary statements of the principles and objectives suggested in a great many of the familiar psychotherapy orientations. Others involve principles actually suggested in only a few orientations and implicitly accepted, ignored, or in some cases even contradicted by other orientations. Orientations might agree on the major objective but suggest their own specific techniques to implement it.

The guidelines serve to draw together and organize procedural considerations of effective eclectic practice, and each is expected to make good sense to a majority of experienced eclectics. The standard for inclusion is not that all the principles are accepted already by everybody, for that would be too limiting, but rather that when properly considered, each should be judged by most eclectics to be important to therapeutic practice.

The approach to psychotherapy suggested by these guidelines is a synthesis of various familiar elements and not necessarily original or unusual in many of its particular features. What is innovative about the approach is the means by which the techniques and procedures are selected, integrated, and shown to make sense together as coordinated elements in a coherent therapeutic practice.

Included in each of the guidelines is the rationale and some suggestions and illustrations of how one can implement the guideline. The aim is to outline guidelines for an integrated eclectic approach and to make them familiar enough to enable one to use them in actual practice. The guidelines are organized into five main categories but are not steps or phases of psychotherapy: each is to be applied across a course of standard therapeutic sessions. The following chapters outline some 25 guidelines for pragmatic practice.

Understanding and Intervention

We face the dual tasks of understanding what goes on, and of intervening to promote changes. In an earlier generation, it was taken for granted that your theoretical viewpoint and your intervention methods would go hand in hand, as a single package. The rationale lost its way, of course, and we now use techniques with little concern for their theoretical origin.[38]

Properly organizing the available interventions allows us to learn them faster, choose them more appropriately, and use them more confidently. Since interventions are the means to accomplish the objectives of therapy, it is most practical to group them by the therapeutic objectives which they are used to attain. That way, interventions can be compared against those with similar uses, and those which are best for your immediate therapeutic objectives can be selected.

Clinical guidelines are used here to organize the action components of psychotherapy. The general objectives for interventions are specified as guidelines, and used to group the techniques from the various schools of therapy.

Truths and Practicalities. Language serves as representation and as action. As representation, language structures observation and stores and transfers information. Statements are judged on whether or not they are so.

Yet language is also action. "Words are also deeds," observes Wittgenstein,39 for in saying something we thereby act to do something, to affect the social situation, to move things along between us. We say things not merely because they are so but in order to get others to hear and to respond. Language philosophers speak of the "speech acts,"40 to remind us that statements are necessarily also actions. So statements are judged also on their aims, their practicality, and their accomplishments.

The action aspect of speech helps make sense of some of the puzzles of language. Words of "love," for instance, refer to an inner feeling or attitude toward a beloved. Yet statements of love are made not merely because they are true and the feeling is experienced, but also for some reason—as a way to do something. One might say "I love you" to a sweetheart, in order to support or reassure, to soothe ruffled feathers, or to court, or maybe to arouse or seduce, or to tender a commitment to the future, or to create in the beloved a sense of obligation, or in anger, to cast blame for not loving sufficiently in return. And conversely, regardless of the feeling, one might avoid words of love to avoid making a personal commitment, or perhaps to avoid appearing weak or vulnerable. Surely, we should not expect to understand much about the meaning of love in our language without understanding the sorts of transactions it is used to conduct.

So too with the words used in therapy sessions. We say things not merely because they are so, but also and necessarily because of their practical contributions to treatment. When what is so conflicts with what is practical to say, we must be careful. As a therapist, it is surely normal to be sympathetic toward our clients, and to try to see in them the most they might be and to reinforce it. One popular technique, positive connotation, reframes or re-describes actions to produce a positive spin, best face forward. Positive connotation might portray a sulker or a scold as deeply in love, although expressing it poorly, suggesting that it is only the confusions of love that lead to the noxious behavior. The reinterpretation might indeed make the individual feel better, at least for awhile, which is one of its objectives. But perhaps the actual reality is a darker spirit, more filled with anger and annoyance than with love. What should be done with that? In being sympathetic, which is surely the natural and practical thing to do, you chance overlooking the unflattering angles which might be important later on.

The balance between the scope of your understanding and the benefits of your intervention must be aligned carefully and rechecked frequently. Just because something is true does not mean that it will be beneficial, but we should avoid things which are untrue, or we are apt to confuse our clients and we will eventually confuse ourselves as well.[41] One of the challenges of doing therapy is to deal with the hard and unflattering material in a practical and supportive manner. The realities of what is so must be blended artfully with the practicalities of how to create changes.

Part II
Guidelines for Interventions

5
The Therapeutic Relationship

The first set of guidelines are general considerations for maintaining a therapeutic relationship.

1. Be respectful
2. Maintain an alliance.
3. Stay credible.
4. Communicate an understanding.
5. Share responsibility for improvement.

Be Respectful

Clients enter therapy and various shapes and sizes and with their own attitudes and beliefs in their own ways of doing things. It is best to accept the ordinary conventions clients bring with them, and to save our challenges for features which are clearly troublesome.

Generally, we would want to make our clients comfortable with us and comfortable with the psychotherapy process. So we should be aware of what clients might see as courtesy, concern, comfort, practical good sense, and so on.

Sometimes respect is conveyed by small things. Being on time to your session conveys respect for your client, while being late conveys lack of concern. If you are late, apologize. If you run late, find out what is going on and fix it.

How much of ourselves should we reveal to our clients? Those who advocate being a "blank screen" and revealing little or nothing about themselves are not being properly neutral, as the original blank screen ideology would have it.. Ordinary conventions hold that the question merits an answer. To fail an answer is not socially neutral but rather is a refusal to answer, and is ordinarily considered arrogant or rude. .

Suppose a client asks "Are you married?" and you say, "That is not our concern here." You are not merely remaining neutral but are rejecting a reasonable request. It is better to answer the question, and get on with things.

How much do clients really want to know about us? Freely answer any appropriate questions about yourself, and you will be surprised about how little clients want to know about you. One or two questions about yourself, and clients go back to their own concerns. Primarily, clients want to know that we understand their problems and that we can help them, and are seldom that interested in the particulars of our lives.

Ordinarily, in conversations, we are expected to share something of ourselves. Those of us who revealed little or nothing of themselves leave clients wondering where they stand and insecure about what they reveal. Be yourself, be involved, contribute, and you will find clients feel relatively secure about you and focus naturally on themselves.

Psychotherapy should be for the benefit of the clients, and only secondarily for the benefit of the therapist, the mental health agency, society, or other parties. The best interests of the client are primary and should be given priority, with few exceptions, over other considerations. See this as a reminder of the importance of maintaining motivations to act in the best interest of the client, and of avoiding or resolving feelings and attitudes contrary to this purpose.

The motivations which therapists should have are easily stated in principle and not always so easily maintained in practice. As psychotherapists we should have feelings and attitudes of acceptance, confidence, comfortableness, compassion, concern, fair play, interest, involvement, practical optimism, respect, stability, and warmth toward our clients; we should avoid, or examine and resolve, feelings and attitudes of aloofness, anger, arrogance, boredom, condemnation, egotism, frustration, guilt, insecurity, and pity toward our clients.

The importance of the positive feelings over the negative ones should be apparent, as interventions made from a positive outlook are generally better than alternative interventions made from the negatives. When our energies are bound up with our own personal issues of anger, frustration, and insecurity, we are not free to give our attention fully to our clients. The importance of positive feelings is emphasized in client-centered, Adlerian, and reality therapy orientations, and is mentioned by other orientations as well. Client-centered therapy prescribes warmth and "unconditional positive regard" for our clients: the "unconditional" means that when the sea gets rough we should not turn foul. Psychoanalytic and psychodynamic training stresses the resolution of "countertransference" reactions, which are our generally negative or inappropriate attitudes and feelings held to be reactions to our patients' misinterpretations of us. The term "countertransference" translates into everyday language as "taking it too personally." In short, client-centered exhorts us to love our clients, and psychodynamic interprets our tendencies to hate them. These two are the flip sides of the same issue.

Although cognitive or behavioral orientations do not emphasize the therapist's attitudes, it would be wrong to conclude that these practitioners are therefore less empathic. The level of warmth and respect behavior therapists have toward their clients is found to beas high as that of client-centered or other therapists who focus more on their relationship to their clients.[42] My own impression, similarly, is that the more active therapists seem to be at least as warm and respectful as the less active ones. Why is it that orientations which do not emphasize their own attitudes and feelings do as well here as those who do focus on these issues?

Troublesome reactions such as anger, frustration, and insecurity are most often generated by the failures of our clients to progress in combination with insinuation against us and resistance to our interventions. Consider that such reactions result from our missing the nuances and from not understanding how to respond effectively. One who is confused and unsure of what to say is easily swayed by feelings of inadequacy, anger, boredom, competitiveness, frustration, and so on. One who sees what has to be done and involves herself in the appropriate interventions is somewhat protected against these adverse feelings. We become more comfortable as we learn to effectively manage the interpersonal difficulties which would otherwise undermine, confuse, and frustrate us.

Those insecurities and frustrations so common in the initial stages of psychotherapy training are too often interpreted as idiosyncratic personality issues of the trainee. As a trainee in a position of responsibility with troubled persons, your insecurities and frustrations are understandable as reactions to your situation, as you are in over your head, and you know it! The main objective of supervision should be to help the trainee to understand the clients and find better ways to intervene with them. Personal feelings should be understood and acknowledged, but individual idiosyncrasies need not be a major focus unless they interfere with the trainee's abilities to learn from supervision.

Unconstructive emotions which do occur find easy expression in an unstructured situation, but are less troublesome when we have guidelines to help structure what we are to be doing and how we go about it.43 The use of intervention guidelines gives us some protection therefore against the effects of unconstructive attitudes and feelings.

Suppose, for instance, that in a first interview with a young man you explore his attitude that other people are stupid, shallow, and only interested in themselves, that they are unimportant, and that he is smart to do without them. It appears to be a good first session, and you mention toward the end of the session that he seems to have dealt with important issues and that you feel he has gotten a good start with them. But the young man comments that it has been a waste of time because you did nothing for him. "What would you know about any of this?" he accuses. "You study your stupid books and get your credentials, but you cannot understand what I am going through. You are just acting interested because that is your job!" The client thus casts you as a boot licker and a fool. How do you respond?

This is the sort of situation which can evoke in a therapist feelings of inadequacy and frustration, as well as anger at the client for his unjust accusation and for his unwillingness to acknowledge the attempt to help. If the therapist should miss the significance of his comments or have no appropriate response, he could easily get caught in these feelings and might act on them in unconstructive ways.

The client in this case casts others as stupid and shallow, and in so doing he does not allow them to be important to him. It is a reasonable bet that he is doing the same thing here with his therapist; so we might respond as follows: "When you see others as so shallow and unimportant, you keep them from becoming too important to you. There are some good reasons for doing that: other people may indeed hurt and disappoint you. Seeing others as unimportant may be your way to keep from getting too involved with them, so that you cannot get hurt by them. You may be concerned here, as well, that if you get involved, it may come to nothing and you will feel hurt and disappointed. That is surely possible, for nothing can be really guaranteed. It seems safer to stay uninvolved with people, but at the same time we do need people, so we cannot really get away from them. It seems you are up against a hard choice here.."

The response shows the sense it makes for the client to see things the way he does and so legitimizes his views. The client, by his comments, has invited an adversary relationship because he challenged and tried to discredit the therapist. It would be easy in such a situation to want to defend ourselves or to fight back. Note here that the therapist does not take his own side in the conflict, but rather takes the client's side. The therapist acts as a supporter and consultant to the client in figuring out his problems with his therapist. The need to stay unentangled with our own positions and to be genuinely committed to our clients is at the heart of the "Be on the client's side" guideline.

Knowing how to interpret and to intervene is essential, for it protects us against unconstructive emotional reactions and generates good feelings. The issue then is not merely to focus on our feelings, but also to involve ourselves in the sorts of interventions which tend to generate good feelings.

The remaining guidelines structure our responses, involve us in constructive and often satisfying tasks, and thereby give us some protection against unconstructive attitudes and feelings. The guidelines can provide some assistance, therefore, in improving our attitudes and feelings about our clients and about doing psychotherapy.

Maintain an alliance

Psychotherapy is most importantly a collaborative activity. The overall aims and objectives are most readily accomplished when therapist and client cooperate together and assist each other, and the maintenance of a cooperative alliance yields real benefits in almost every aspect of the therapeutic process. It is important and in some ways essential, therefore, that we act as allies and that our clients come to see and to accept us as allies.

The client's experience of an ally is in itself therapeutic, it is generally agreed, for the sense that the therapist is accepting and supportive conveys that the client is an acceptable and worthwhile individual and that he matters to someone of some significance. It also invites the client to identify with and perhaps emulate the therapist's supportiveness and strengths, and thus learn to better manage his own interpersonal relationships.

An alliance is also an important condition for further influence since it enables a therapist to effectively utilize a range of candid or forceful interventions which would otherwise lead only to trouble: it enables us to gain leverage from interpretations and suggestions which would otherwise cause argument and resistance. Suppose that a therapist comments, "Might I hazard a guess that you are sometimes more than just a little bit stubborn?" to a client adhering obstinately to an untenable position. If the therapist is already seen as an ally, this has a good chance of evoking from the client a smile of recognition and some inclination perhaps to consider further the issue of stubbornness. But if the therapist is viewed as an antagonist, the interpretation stands to be seen as an uncomplimentary insinuation which may evoke argument, resistance, and further stubbornness. As a general axiom, one is more inclined to accept hard truths and difficult suggestions from someone who is seen as an ally. One is on guard and often opposes as unfriendly intrusions these same comments from someone who is seen as an adversary.

Client-centered, humanistic, analytic, object relations, and psychodynamic orientations see the client's relationship to the therapist as itself therapeutic, while behavioral orientations see it mainly as an instrument for effective influence. We do not have to choose between these positions: it is both.

. All indications are that expectations for progress should be markedly lowered for clients who are unable to see their therapists as allies.44 The establishment of an alliance thus has high priority. To establish an alliance, we act as an ally to the client-as a supporter, a confidante, a consultant, and a collaborator. Furthermore, we must act in ways that enable the clients to see us as allies. Some principles for doing this are suggested here.

Begin where you are welcome. Particular problems may involve issues which are relatively safe, and other issues which are threatening and uncomfortable. It is best in such cases to begin with those issues in which you are seen most easily as an ally, and to save for the moment those issues in which your position is open to misinterpretation.

One woman, for instance, continually mismanages and screams at her children, and condemns herself relentlessly for her failings as a mother. The situation allows one to begin either with the child management issues or with the self-condemnation. It is better to begin where you are most readily seen as an ally, for instance: "It is not going as well as you would want with your children, and you condemn and harass yourself for each and every failing. You are so tough on yourself, it seems, that it would be difficult for you to feel comfortable at all with your children and to enjoy being with them. The excessive self-condemnation may be itself a major element in your problems, for it prevents you from doing your best. Let's begin there-shall we?-and see what we can figure out."

An attempt to begin instead by suggesting better child management procedures would run a good chance here of failure. The woman is too touchy, and would too easily interpret any suggestions as further evidence that she has done things wrong and that she has indeed ruined her children by her many mistakes.

The mother begins in an impossible position-both wanting to improve as a parent and unable to tolerate the existing failings in herself. An initial focus on the self-condemnation shows a sensitivity to her position, and establishes the therapist as a supporter and an ally. It is easier then from the position of an ally to deal with the complex issues of better child management.

The same issues are seen again in a second illustration: A young woman is excessively invested in, and continually upset by, her relationship with her mother. Both daughter and mother appear to be contributing equally to the general malaise, for each deals with the other in the same underhanded and manipulative manner: each uses upsetness and sulking to intimidate and gain advantage over the other. The situation thus allows one to begin either with the young woman's manipulativeness or with the ways in which she is herself manipulated by her mother. The "whose side are you on?" issue is critical in these sorts of situations, and it is best to begin where you are most readily seen as an ally, for example: "Your mom continually shows you how miserable her life is and how much you upset her when you do not comply with her wishes. The implication is that your mother's feelings are entirely your responsibility, and that you are a rotten person and it is entirely your fault when she is so upset. . . . Is all that upsetness really authentic? Do you ever wonder if she uses it to make you feel guilty and to manipulate you into doing what she wants?"

An attempt to begin instead by showing the young woman that she is herself manipulative would invite unnecessary difficulties. The mother contends that the daughter is at fault in the relationship, and an initial interpretation of the daughter's manipulativeness would appear as agreement with the mother's position. The young woman would see the interpretation as yet another accusation and would see the therapist as yet another adversary.

In beginning as he does with the unfair influences against the client, the therapist thus establishes himself as a supporter and an ally. It is easier then as an ally to interpret the young woman's own manipulative contributions. The issue of influencing through being upset is already understood and can be used in the next step: "As a youngster growing up, you learned naturally enough from your mom that being upset and refusing to speak are the effective ways to gain advantage in an argument. It is understandable enough that you too learned to use that strategy in order to hold your own against your mom. As a youngster, you saw no other ways available to you . . . As an adult, you are now in a much better position. Let's look at some more effective ways of holding your own with your mother, which do not involve investing in that same old pattern."

The interpretation thus legitimizes the young woman's current manipulative patterns, for it shows that they were acquired honestly: the manipulative tendencies are now seen as understandable reactions to ongoing manipulations and not merely as indications of bad character. The therapist thus establishes an alliance by his initial support against the mother's unfair manipulations and he maintains the alliance by legitimizing the daughter's own similar manipulative strategies.

Maintaining an alliance is a first priority. We focus initially on establishing an alliance, and then continue with other objectives in ways which tend to further the alliance and with an eye out for signs of trouble. Should some of our interventions seriously weaken our alliance, then we must soften or alter the intervention, and take measures to repair any damage and to reestablish the alliance.

Sessions with several family members present introduce the sometimes troublesome requirement that we maintain an alliance with each of the often antagonistic intimates. One writer suggests that the adult who is less involved with the problem be spoken to first, and the person with the most power to bring the family back be treated with the most concern and respect. Often we can maintain alliances with each of several quarreling family members by understanding and legitimizing each of their positions, and by working for fair play and equitable compromises.

Counter Transference! Clients who have felt neglected or mistreated in other important relationships may anticipate the same or similar mistreatment in their relationship with their therapists. Some tendency to see a therapist as too similar to a parent or other intimate is only natural and has been termed "transference" in psychoanalytic parlance. The tendency is easily understandable from a general principle: a person takes the world to be as he has found it, so he expects to be treated as he has been treated in previous similar situations. Such misinterpretations weaken the therapeutic alliance and impede constructive collaboration. We should act to minimize transference reactions, and should troubleshoot and intervene to counter transference reactions which do occur. To maintain an alliance we must counter transference.

One client is initially guarded and uncooperative: he gives only minimal comments, and those in response to questions, and he withholds anything important about himself. One gets the initial impression that he is mistrustful of the therapist and of the relationship. The following is an attempt to troubleshoot the problem:

Therapist: You give little or no information on your own, and only the minimum when I share my thoughts or ask questions. It seems that maybe you are feeling that you do not entirely trust me, or you are wondering if I might have some advantage over you if you do say too much about yourself.

Client: Well, maybe. It takes me a while to open up, I guess.

Therapist: Have you had some experiences where you have told someone about yourself and found that he or she used it against you?

Client: No, not really.

Therapist: Never? Has there not been maybe a time when someone understood you, and used this to criticize or manipulate? Your parents, for instance, how do you get along with them?

Client: I get along with them OK now, I guess.

Therapist: And when you were growing up?

Client: Well, my father was unhappy a lot of the time, and moody.

Therapist: And how did he treat you?

Client: When he was frustrated, he would yell at me, often for things I could not really do anything about. I felt criticized a lot, I guess. I remember that I would stay out of the way, and not say anything, because I was afraid of making him angry.

Therapist: So you learned quite naturally that some people cannot be trusted, and you learned to stay back until you find out a bit more about whom you are dealing with.... It makes some sense to do that here as well, at least until you find out more about me and about how I respond to the information you do offer.... Gradually, I expect, you will find that there are at least a few differences between me and your father.

Client (laughs): There are a few differences, for sure.

The young man was expecting about the same treatment from the therapist as he had received from his father and was responding in one of the ways he had learned to respond in such situations. The therapist's initial comments are attempts to understand and to legitimize the fellow's guardedness and reluctant participation. Since no explanations had been volunteered, the therapist's initial comments are necessarily estimates of what might be going on. These comments are attempts to understand and legitimize the problem: although sometimes incorrect, they come across nonetheless as supportive and so cast the therapist as an ally. The therapist in these interpretations shows that he can understand and accept the young man's minimal participation; thus he contrasts in this important way with the moody and often critical father.

As a principle, we should clarify the actual relationship, and establish sufficient contrast between ourselves and the parties in those other relationships which are seen as so unsatisfactory. Many schools are in agreement here, notably Adlerians, who are themselves anything but anonymous; reality therapists, whose first principle is to be personable to the clients; and family therapists, who bring those other contrasting relationships into the therapy sessions. The psychoanalytic and psychodynamic traditions straddle the fence, in that classical analytic practice encourages transference-and so stands in opposition-whereas the current psychodynamic practice which emphasizes reconstructive emotional experiences and the early resolution of transference is thus in agreement.

The rationale in classical analytic practice is that transference must be encouraged so that it may be explored and analyzed at length, and, through the course of analysis, resolved. The analyst remains anonymous-a so-called "blank screen"-and thus invites in the patient fantasies and misinterpretations, which occur unfortunately in confused combination with realistic anger and insecurities over being unsupported and ignored. Advocates of encouraging transference note the importance of a working alliance, but they assume rather uncritically that one can both encourage transference reactions and at the same time maintain the stability of a working alliance. The plausibility of a client's seeing a therapist as a critical and abandoning father figure and at the same time as an accepting and trustworthy ally stretches the imagination. It is possible to alternate between suspicion and trust, but the client cannot have a full measure of each of them at the same time.

We must choose, therefore, between encouraging transference or maintaining an alliance. An average client already has more than his share of what he perceives as unsupportive or otherwise unsatisfactory relationships and does not need one more with his therapist. When we are seen as supportive and trustworthy, we stand in contrast and are in a better position to explore those other relationships and to promote more satisfactory ways of relating. As a general principle: In order to counter transference, be personable and participate actively, and interpret and challenge transference reactions which do occur.

The principles and guidelines here are general considerations for practice and not particular techniques which can be memorized and performed blindly. We must weave the guidelines appropriately into the ongoing therapeutic procedure. The means by which we try to maintain an alliance may be complex and quite varied, and may call upon the full sensitivity and experience of the individual practitioner. Nor is it always possible to form an alliance, for some clients remain suspicious and uncooperative in spite of our best efforts.

Any number of additional principles and considerations may be involved in maintaining an alliance. The issues of maintaining and utilizing an alliance continue to weave through our remaining assortment of therapeutic guidelines, and several additional principles will be presented which serve to cast us as allies.

Stay Credible

Being seen by the client as competent and sensible contributes measurably to the impact of our interpretations and suggestions and, therefore, to our overall effectiveness as therapists. A number of considerations improve our credibility with our clients and thereby help maintain our opportunities to influence them.

Showing the sensibleness of our interpretations and suggestions provides a good beginning. Clients deserve an explanation anyway, and a well-communicated rationale for what we are doing instills confidence in the programs we undertake. Psychotherapy need not be a secretive or esoteric procedure which is conducted on clients without their understanding. Indeed, clients are generally appreciative when we share with them the secrets of what we are attempting to accomplish, and are in a better position from there to collaborate and contribute. Some evidence indicates that physicians who explain the medical problems and procedures inspire greater cooperation and confidence in their patients than those who attempt to maintain their credibility as experts through looking important and keeping the information to themselves. The principle is clear enough, and we in counseling and psychotherapy need only to heed the lesson.

Explaining our rationales does not lock us to them or require that we never change our minds or never acknowledge misdirections. When we do change directions, we can explain whatever new considerations are operative so that the changes make sense, and such changes are generally accepted with few problems. Changing as we consider things further may itself improve our credibility because clients, like anyone else, have more respect for those who are flexible than for those who consider themselves infallible. Also, acknowledging misdirections may give the client a needed invitation to do so himself without undue strains on pride and ego.

Our ideas need not always be better than those of our clients, for a cooperative give-and-take with our clients speaks well of our flexibility and good sense. Competitiveness and one-upmanship with our clients over who is right are clearly out of line.

Oftentimes clients find themselves feeling better, but do not see the connections to the seemingly minor changes that we have worked on with them. When our interventions result in improvements, it is good to link the two together in the client's mind, both to establish the credibility of our programs and to further motivate the client to continue with them. Thus to one who is feeling better we might comment: "Be sure to note that you started feeling better shortly after you made those important stands with your husband; and that when you did that earlier you felt better, and when you forgot to do it you started feeling worse again. The things we are working on do make a difference, and it is important to stay with them."

Some long term orientations are wary of providing quick relief for fear that the client who is no longer suffering will not be sufficiently motivated to work on the more fundamental characterological problems. The suggestion here, in contrast, is to attack first those problems which appear easiest in order to gain leverage and improve things. Showing that our programs really can and do improve things improves our credibility immeasurably, and generally increases rather than decreases the willingness of clients to stay with therapy. Those who do choose to leave with the quick fix at least know that we know how to do something which works. We invite them back should further problems occur, and we have not really lost those clients either.

Explaining expected problems or relapses prior to their occurrence helps maintain the credibility of our programs. Along with suggestions for parents to more strictly manage their troublesome youngster, we might explain that he will be mad about it and fight them, and may look considerably worse before he looks better. If this were not explained, then the youngster's objections and escalating troublesomeness would be taken as indications that our therapeutic program is wrong and has failed. However, the same problems, explained and even predicted in advance, can be cast instead as further confirmation that we know what goes on and that the program is working as expected.

If we were to say things which are untruthful and get caught at it, then that quite obviously would undermine our credibility. The ways in which our clients interpret our comments matter considerably, for saying things which appear to be untruthful or wrong can undermine our credibility every bit as much as saying things which actually are wrong. As therapists, we introduce new ideas, and we explore and weigh them with our clients so that they can attain more realistic understandings. Ideas too far from what our clients accept already can overshoot the mark and result in the clients' discrediting our statements rather than changing their opinions. Some cautions are in order therefore against committing ourselves to statements which are correct in fact but which we cannot get our clients to see as anything but wrong.

Those clients convinced of their own worthlessness who cannot accept those who approve of them present for us a subtle problem in maintaining our own credibility. Include here those who are convinced they are stupid, ugly, bizarre, trashy, or in any of the range of ways worthless and socially unacceptable, and who cannot and will not accept any opinion contrary to their own convictions. One who is so thoroughly convinced of his flaws does not consider the opinions of others who try to reassure him that he is intelligent, attractive, or an otherwise acceptable human being. A classic Groucho Marx quip portrays the position well, along the lines that: "I would never belong to any country club that would have the likes of me as a member." Any club unselective enough to accept him thereby discredits itself in his eyes. A person such as this figures that others who try to reassure him either see his flaws, but are pretending otherwise as a social courtesy, or do not see his flaws because they are naive and gullible or because he has fooled them for the moment into seeing him as normal. Either way their statements count for nothing because those who are nice as a courtesy do not really believe their own words, while those whom he has fooled will find out sooner or later about his awful character and the charade will be exposed. He discredits as false or naive the reassurance he receives, and discredits similarly those who attempt to reassure and support him.

The only relationships these persons accept as genuine are antagonistic ones because antagonists, they feel, see their undesirableness and are real enough to treat them accordingly. Such persons frequently wallow in abusive relationships and are too easily mislabeled masochistic. The person is not there because he loves pain, but rather because like anyone else he is more comfortable with those he feels are being real with him.

As therapists we act generally as allies and supporters, but the subtle problem here is that in appearing supportive with these clients, we would seem false or naive and discredit ourselves in their eyes. The requirement then is that we be supportive while skirting the problem of discrediting ourselves by appearing naively supportive. With an intelligent young man who is convinced that he is fundamentally stupid, for instance, we cannot merely reassure him or even point to the good marks he makes in graduate school, for those were flukes and anyway he has the instructors fooled too: he is really an impostor masquerading as a smart student. But conversely, it would be wrong to agree with him that he is stupid, for he is not and there are traps waiting for one who argues untruths. Remaining silent is also not a good option, however, because by remaining silent one fails to be supportive and comes across either as above it or as stuck, which is not helpful. So where do we go? What we can do is clarify and legitimize the client's position, and from there avoid being caught by it and perhaps move on to challenge it.

We clarify the inclination to discredit supporters as a first step to enable the client to accept support. We might mention the Groucho Marx quip and draw the parallels: "Groucho Marx said that he would never belong to any club that would have him as a member. You are a lot like Groucho and the country club—-you discredit anyone who is undiscerning enough to accept you." The particulars must be elaborated and the problem hashed through as much as is necessary. Once the problem has been clarified, we can use it to cover ourselves when we are being overtly supportive, as in the following compliment: "Actually you are doing quite well, but if I were to tell you that you would lose respect for my judgment." It is a compliment, but it stays one jump ahead of the client's tendency to discredit: in the same motion, we make the pitch and cover the bases.

We might also interpret the client's tendencies to present himself as so stupid: perhaps he does this to avoid the possibility of being disappointed, or to evoke reassurance and involvement from his friends, or for other reasons. We legitimize and make sense of those tendencies, and only then go on to challenge. By clarifying the inclinations to discredit, we remain credible ourselves and so remain in a position to be taken seriously.

One who argues forcefully that he is stupid makes an obvious contradiction, and we might challenge that, as by saying: "Everyone argues that you are plenty smart enough, but you are sure that you really know you are stupid and they do not. For one who sees himself as so stupid, you sure have a lot of confidence in your opinion. I realize you are arguing that you are inferior, but you come across as quite sure of yourself: you are sure that you are right on this and that nobody else knows anything at all." The comment is challenging in appearance but supportive in substance. Because it is challenging, the client cannot assume we are just being nice to him or that he has us fooled; yet the thrust of the interpretation is that there is more to him than he is admitting.

Ostensibly the client has an inferiority complex, but note the shades of superiority and aloofness in one who discredits so easily those who appear supportive. One who ostensibly sees himself as so inferior nonetheless remains in charge of his attitudes and has the satisfaction of feeling superior to those who are so foolish as to accept him. In interpreting the control he exercises, we accredit the client as someone in charge already of one critical aspect of his life-a principle elaborated in later guidelines.

Those who are reserved and aloof maintain their status as objective observers above the client but are not sufficiently supportive, while those who are too overtly supportive offer something important but chance being discredited in the process. The artistry is in being supportive and remaining credible at the same time. The credibility of the healer is suggested by Jerome Frank as an essential factor to all forms of psychological treatment, and credibility is emphasized as a major factor in attitude change in the social psychological approach to treatment [45]

Share your understanding

An individual's feelings and concerns are too often overlooked or misunderstood in ongoing, everyday communications. One who understands and acknowledges another's position shows an interest and concern, and is seen more readily as an ally and a supporter. It is important then for a therapist to convey that he does understand and accept the important aspects of the client's communications.

Specific techniques for expressing one's understanding are emphasized in client-centered and related counseling orientations, and in parenting communications training. These techniques are variously termed empathic responding by Rogers, reflective listening by Haim Ginott,[46] and active listening by Thomas Gordon[47]. Any of these terms seems satisfactory.

The main principle is to listen carefully to the feelings and concerns being communicated, and then to share our understanding of the important elements. An empathic listening response may grasp key words or phrases, but it should not be a mere paraphrase of the person's statement. Any response qualifies which adequately conveys that we understand and accept the important feelings and concerns.

Empathic listening responses convey understanding and acceptance, but they should not imply agreement on anything which appears inaccurate or false. Suppose a woman expresses strong anger over the way her husband is treating her; compare the following empathic responses:

1. "You feel he is being really unfair, and you find yourself angry over the way he is treating you."

2. "Sounds like he is being quite inconsiderate and unfair, and you are really angry about it."

The first acknowledges the sense of injustice and anger, and the second includes agreement that the sense of mistreatment is accurate and realistic. Both convey an understanding of the client's position, for we need not be in agreement in order to convey understanding and acceptance. We can express an understanding even when the client's position seems problematic. But only when the client's position appears accurate and appropriate should our response include agreement.

An empathic response may sometimes pass over a manifest question, and focus instead on the implicit issues and concerns which are being expressed. A mother, for instance, asks anxiously about her troubled youngster: "I want to know if I am the cause of the problems he is having." A good response is: "Sounds like you are feeling responsible, and you are wondering if you are to blame for literally everything that is going wrong." The response makes explicit the underlying concern and suggests an important issue for further consideration. The initial question the mother asked may be answered as well, if it remains important. But the major focus should be on what appear to be the primary issues and problems conveyed in the client's communication.

Empathic statements may help clarify the issues for client and therapist alike: empathic responses focus the client's attention on impor-

tant aspects of his feelings and concerns, encourage him to understand and accept aspects which otherwise may have been overlooked or avoided, and tend to increase the richness and complexity with which he understands himself and his relationships. Empathic responses also focus the therapist's attention on understanding better what is being communicated and give us an opportunity to improve our understanding as a client confirms or questions our initial impressions. Empathic listening tends to facilitate further client communication: it conveys an interest in what the client is saying, and it helps us avoid asking too many questions or giving easy advice based on too little understanding.

Showing that we understand should not be seen as incompatible in any way with any of the range of further interventions. The sequencing of therapeutic interventions is important. One who acknowledges another's position is more easily seen as an ally, and is in a better position from there to challenge and restructure. Expressing an understanding is thus an initial intervention which prepares the groundwork for later, more forceful strategies for change. In general, as each issue is introduced, we should convey that we understand the client's position on that issue, and then continue from there to interpretation and redirection.

The empathic response is given an exalted position in classical client-centered counseling: it is the answer to everything, and anything else a counselor might do is just plain wrong. Most eclectics use empathic responses but reject the restrictive ideology. We see the empathic response as but one of a range of available therapeutic responses.

Empathic communication is thus an initial therapeutic response which encourages an alliance, clarifies issues, opens communication, and thereby prepares the groundwork for further, more forceful or elaborate therapeutic interventions. Empathic statements are those recurring nickle-and-dime interventions which each contribute only a smidgen of therapeutic movement, but without which the course of therapeutic progress would be markedly slower.

Share responsibility for improvement.

Psychotherapy is a collaborative activity in which client and therapist both contribute: each should share, therefore, in the responsibility fo making things go as they should. By everyday conventions, some measure of responsibility is generally assigned to each of the participants in any collaborative activity, and we build here upon these commonsense conventions.

Being responsible for something involves the complementary aspects of being in charge and of being accountable. These two aspects usually go together, since one who is in charge of something stands to be held accountable for the outcome. Sharing responsibility thus involves sharing control of the activity and also sharing accountability for the results. As therapists we take control so that our clients learn to better control their own lives, and we emphasize compassion and openness to learn rather than condemnation as we assess our own accountability. Some practitioners avoid taking control for fear of taking control away from the client, or to avoid being accountable. Issues of control and accountability are dealt with here in turn.

It is common for clients to fail to take responsibility for their lives, and to contend instead that it is others who are causing the problems and who should be expected therefore to provide the solutions. Such persons do not seek cooperative solutions. Instead, through passivity, misery, resentment, and accusation, they attempt to transfer the full responsibility to others. "It's up to you, not me" is their attitude and also their intended message. An inability to accept responsibility is itself a major limitation, for it undermines self-initiative and impedes any collaborative efforts to seek solutions.

It may be tempting for a therapist to counter the "it's up to you" attitude through a similarly passive "no, it is up to you" attitude of his own. A client who refuses to accept responsibility thereby invites the therapist to take over. In remaining passive, the therapist foils the invitation, thus forcing the client to take some initiative or to endure the silence. A passive stance is therefore a means to avoid accepting the wrong sorts of responsibility. It is generally ineffective, however, as a long run approach. Passivity by a

80

therapist leaves the client feeling unsupported and thus further impairs the already fragile therapeutic alliance. Troubled clients, furthermore, are not merely unwilling but generally and in important ways unable to take appropriate responsibility. A passive countermove is therefore counterproductive, for neither therapist nor client generates solutions, and both are stranded together in a muddle of entangling inactivity.

It is better in such cases to deal actively with the issues of responsibility, as in the following illustration. A young woman complains about her marriage–her husband neglects her and refuses either to acknowledge his contributions to the problem or to make the changes she requires. The therapist tries to explore some obvious alternatives: she might consider ways to adapt herself to the marriage, try on her own to improve the relationship, or leave. But the woman is uninterested in any of these alternatives. Her husband is making her life impossible, she contends, and it is intolerably unfair therefore that she should be expected to have to make the changes; it is up to him, and not her, to make the necessary changes.

She also brings the same attitude into her approach to her therapy. She is uninterested in changing herself and is waiting for the therapist to redress the gross unfairness that life has perpetrated upon her: it is not up to her but up to her therapist to make things better for her. This woman is entrapped by her failure to take responsibility and has only the vaguest understanding of her self-generated bondage. There are two separate but related problems, one in her understanding and the other in the thrust of her actions. She misconstrues and overestimates her husband's contributions, for although he contributes to the problems, she contributes also, so that he is certainly not the sole cause which she has convinced herself he is. The thrust of her actions is more subtle and complex but extremely important: she is attempting to make him responsible; to do so, she presents herself as miserable, accuses him of causing her problems, remains passive, refuses to try to

81

change herself, and thus commits herself to the miseries she claims he is causing. Her objectives are to show him he cannot get away with neglecting her, to make him feel responsible for her feelings, and to force him to become more considerate. Her objectives are understandable enough, but her use of miserableness is not particularly effective and carries too high a price. As a means of getting him to be more responsible, it is clearly cost ineffective.

There are any number of ways to begin to intervene, such as: "You have issues of whether he should change and issues of how to get him to change, and you must distinguish between the two. We can both agree that he is contributing to the problems and that therefore he should change, for a husband should be more involved and considerate. But you have yet to deal with the issue of whether he will change and what you might do to get him to change." The comment distinguishes between ethical questions as opposed to practical means

to improve the situation. Agreement here that the husband should make some change conveys supportiveness and casts the therapist as an ally: although certainly not the whole story, it is nonetheless a place to begin. The means by which the husband actually might change is presented then as a separate and further issue.

Perhaps the husband is most annoyed by her continual upset and ongoing insinuation that it is all his responsibility, so that an improvement in the wife's attitude might yield real improvement in the entire marriage. The therapist explores these relationship factors and suggests how she might contribute to a solution, but she is too committed to her current position to accept the reinterpretation. The impasse continues.

We might better focus on the pragmatics of the wife's statements. The "you are responsible" messages to her husband are attempts to force him to accept the responsibility; thus, the following intervention: "In holding your husband responsible, you invite him to take responsibility and to treat you better. Your premise, it seems, is something like this: `If only I could make him see how upset he is making me, then he would feel responsible, and he would have to treat me better, as he should.'" Once the woman understands and acknowledges her approach, then the issue of its effectiveness can be raised: "Is your strategy going to work?" The outline provides a beginning, and we might elaborate and expand on the themes.

Suppose that further conversation reveals that this woman grew up with parents who were overconcerned with her feelings and who took responsibility themselves for her every unhappiness. The information can be used to further understand and legitimize the pattern: "When you got upset as a youngster, your mom and dad would do almost anything to make you feel better. You learned naturally enough that when things go wrong, it is someone else's responsibility to make you feel better, and all you need to do is to show them how upset they have made you. Your problem here is that your husband does not react to you the same way your parents react. When you get upset and angry, your husband does not take responsibility. Rather, he becomes annoyed and ignores you even more. It seems as though the rules have changed, and nobody told you. You were taught that being upset gets you some cooperation, and now here it does not. That must seem unfair.

The experience as a youngster thus makes more understandable the woman's pattern of being upset and moody, and of requiring someone else to make things better. It also enables the woman to see better why her current approach is a failure, for the rules have changed and she did not notice it. In acknowledging the apparent unfairness, the therapist appeals to her belief that things are unfair and thereby makes it easier for her to accept the interpretation. When she understands, it is no longer so easy to continue the same blind pattern. Holding others responsible thus loses some of its appeal, and she becomes more inclined then to look for other alternatives.

Note in this case that the therapist takes responsibility in order to enable the client to take responsibility. To share responsibility we take responsibility in ways that enable the client to begin to take responsibility himself, but not in ways that take away responsibility. We do this most readily not through remaining passive, but through various courses of active interventions.

Note also that the therapist adapts and alters strategies to gain the appropriate impact. It is not sufficient to conduct a standard therapeutic approach and to make it the responsibility of the client to benefit from it. When a client fails to benefit from one approach, we should make it our responsibility as therapists to figure out the problems and to change and implement alternative approaches. We need to tailor interventions to fit the particular inclinations and abilities of each individual client.

A client unwilling to take responsibility generates a major problem, but not necessarily an insurmountable one. Some argue that the client has to really want to change and thus hold the client accountable, but that is too simplistic and notoriously ineffective. A troubled individual who is unwilling to change is also in some important manner unable to change. Our task, as in the case just described, is to figure out why the person is unable to change and to address the issues involved. It is our responsibility as therapists to enable the client to better assume responsibility for his own life.

Managing issues of responsibility in therapy is often quite challenging, for there are complexities and considerable room to wrangle over who is responsible for each particular aspect. We try to contribute that which the client is unable to contribute, and we invite and require a client to contribute in every way he is able. Therapist and client must complement and assist each other.

Being responsible involves being in charge, and it also means being accountable; thus blame and recrimination are possible when things go wrong. It is this latter issue of accountability and recrimination which makes responsibility so uncomfortable and troublesome. Many clients may avoid taking charge of their lives in order to avoid being accountable. Should we not recognize that therapists too might avoid being in charge of therapy sessions in order to avoid being accountable for the outcomes?

In my own training, I consulted with a schoolteacher to help her more effectively manage an extremely difficult and unruly class of students. The consultation was ineffective because of the inherent difficulty of the class, the inflexibility of this particular teacher, and my own limited abilities as a consultant trainee. Imagine the worst possible outcome of such a situation: over a Christmas vacation the teacher committed suicide, leaving fellow teachers, students, and others involved to figure it out as best we could. While the main impetus appeared post mortem to be loneliness and adversities in her family relationships, the daily frustrations of that unmanageable class undoubtedly worsened the situation. I was devastated and, in what I now realize is a typical reaction, I indulged myself in feelings of inadequacy, guilt, and self-recrimination over what I should or could have done but failed to do.

I sought my training supervisors for assistance and support. A first supervisor listened briefly to the situation and then told me that I was not responsible: it was a situation over which I had no control, and the teacher as an adult and professional was responsible for her own actions. Students, he concluded, always take these things far too personally. While the information may have been correct, it was not particularly helpful. I surely felt responsible, and those feelings could not be ignored.

A second training supervisor listened carefully to the situation, and then commented that I did indeed share some responsibility, as did everyone else involved, but that my own responsibility was probably much less than I was imagining it to be. What I needed to do for myself was to sort through the extent to which I was and was not responsible, and to find some reconciliation which I could live with. That I found was extremely helpful. In my inventory, I noted that I was merely a consultant and not a therapist. A consultant, according to the approach we were learning, does not intervene in the teacher's personal affairs, for if he does he is soon seen as an in-house shrink and is excluded by other teachers from their classroom concerns. Nevertheless, the issue was still emotionally laden. I explained to a third supervisor that I was only a consultant, and therefore it was not really as bad as if I had been her therapist and had been intimately involved with her personal issues. "It's even worse," he replied, and I held onto my chair as I felt my foundations give way. "Because then you didn't even get a chance to try to help." This last comment rearranged my views of responsibility for the better. There can be actual satisfactions in the willing acceptance of responsibility, even without guarantee of a favorable outcome.

It is too easy to assume that by being less involved we are thereby less accountable when things go poorly. Active involvement is advocated here, and thoughtful attempts to assist by whatever means are appropriate. "Share responsibility" implies that we share accountability, but it is not a recipe for self-recrimination when things go wrong. We need to see ourselves as accountable, but in ways which avoid excessive self-recrimination for mistakes and failures. We must rely on compassion and gentleness toward ourselves, and on an openness to learn by our mistakes. In so doing, we convey by example an important lesson in responsibility: we show that it is possible to be committed and involved, and to be nonetheless accepting of oneself when things go wrong.

"Share responsibility" is suggested here as a guideline for effective collaboration, and responsibility is apportioned on the basis of practical considerations. We are to take charge in ways that move things forward, and to place our clients in charge in ways that they are able to manage. We should hold ourselves accountable to the extent that it is within our reach to make changes and hold our clients accountable when that would benefit them. Likewise, we do not hold our clients accountable when they are overly conscientious already and would be overwhelmed by further accountability.

The guideline to share responsibility comes from considerations of therapeutic impact. Telling a client "you are responsible" is not merely a statement of existing realities, for words are deeds, and telling someone he is responsible is usually a way of holding him responsible. This we should do when it moves things forward and not otherwise.

The issue of responsibility for psychotherapy is often approached from one or the other of two supposedly competing positions. One position, seen commonly in analytic, psychodynamic, client-centered, humanistic, and existential approaches, is that the client is responsible for session gains because it is he who must choose his course and who must live finally with the consequences of his own actions. The contrasting position, seen commonly in behavioral and inmany family systems orientations, is that the therapist is responsible because we are the ones who are engaged to find solutions which the client on his own is unable to manage. Communications strategist Jay Haley is widely appreciated for his tongue-in-cheek satire on professionals who abdicate responsibility for therapeutic progress. The guideline here draws from the two positions, although somewhat greater importance is given to the responsibility of the therapist.

In taking our share of the responsibility, we cast ourselves as allies, for we actively collaborate with the client in seeking solutions. The remaining guidelines are ways of taking our share of the responsibility for therapeutic impact.

6
Affirmation and Accreditation

Their confusions, inadequacies, and failures are all too obvious, and most clients emphasize these and fail to see the many strengths they might have which exist alongside their problems. The person who sees few or no strengths in himself faces a sadly unmanageable task: How does one make oneself into an adequate person when there is so very little to work with? It is not surprising that so many lose heart or never attempt the struggles of psychotherapy in the first place. One of our major initial tasks is to introduce and affirm your client's existing strengths so that these can be acknowledged, accepted, and used as a more suitable basis for realistic attempts to improve existing inadequacies.

The following guidelines are to affirm existing strengths and to accredit the client as someone who already makes sense, is acceptable, and in important ways is in control of his own life:

Legitimize (show the client the sense she makes).
Make it acceptable.
Confirm the client's control.
Don't buy victim acts.
If it works, don't fix it.

Legitimize (Show the client the sense he or she makes)

There are ways in which clients are rational and make sense, and ways in which they are confused and mistaken. We have choices, therefore, as therapists on where we begin and what we emphasize. There are important reasons to begin with the ways our clients do make sense, and to use these as a foundation to troubleshoot and resolve the mistakes and errors. To legitimize, as used here, is to show the client the sense he or she makes.

The importance of legitimizing is seen over and over in almost every clinical issue we encounter. In one case, a man complains bitterly that his wife does not care enough for him to fulfill his legitimate needs, that other women he has known have not given him what he needs, and that more generally life itself is niggardly and unfair to him. From other things he says, however, it appears that his wife is reasonably concerned with him, and that while she does not give everything, she does give considerably more than he acknowledges and as much as might be reasonably expected with so little appreciation. The therapist mentions some of those things she does contribute to him, but he argues the more strongly that she gives him nothing at all, or nothing of real importance. Thus, he is grossly mistaken in how little he is being given and critically restricted in his ability to appreciate any of the good things that life is offering him.

We cannot merely continue to suggest that women can be nurturing and supportive or that he should appreciate what women give him, for he argues the more strongly that it is not so. We must challenge, but before challenging it, we must understand the sense it makes. He wants more from women, and as we explore further, it becomes clear that he feels that since women give him so little, they owe him more and should be expected to give him more. He continually complains and is unappreciative in order to show the inequity and thus require women to treat him better. To maintain his position he discredits anything he is given, so that he experiences himself as receiving nothing and thereby further confirms his argument.

Our intervention is to legitimize his position: "You want more from women, and by arguing that women give you nothing at all, you are making a case that you have been mistreated and that they owe you something better than that.

You make this argument in order to get a woman to see your side and to realize that she should treat you better. It seems that if she could only see how little she is giving, then fair is fair, and she would realize that she better give you the things you really need. The flip side of this is that if you were to acknowledge and appreciate the things that you are already getting, then she would no longer be obligated to you, and you would have to settle and not get anything else. So that leaves you with no reason to appreciate her, and lots of reason not to."

After showing the sense it makes, we can go on to better challenge the misconception: "The argument makes some sense, for there are those times when you have to really justify yourself to get anything. But not always, and in this case the argument is failing to get you anywhere. Sometimes it works the other way around. As you do appreciate what you are given you receive more, because others want to give more when they are appreciated and because you are more open to what is given. And as you fail to appreciate you receive less, because others tire of hearing all the complaints and so they give even less, and you are closed to whatever is given. . . ." "With many women it works just backwards from the way you were figuring it works, which would explain why you are winding up with so very little.... " "Appreciating what your wife gives would not mean settling for less, as you figure it would. My best bet is that it would encourage her, and you would find yourself getting much much more."

Perhaps this man grew up in a family in which he was ignored most of the time and only got his share of anything when he complained loudly enough to intimidate his mother. We might use that information to legitimize his unconstructive pattern: "When you were growing up things did work that way, for by complaining enough you obligated your mother to do things for you; otherwise, you were ignored. Naturally, you might take for granted that it works that way with other women as well and continue with what you learned to do. But what works in one situation does not always work in another,

90

and your wife does not respond the same way your mother did."

His operating premise here is that by arguing how unfair a woman is, he justifies himself and forces her to give him more. By showing him the sense in his position, we construct a framework from which its inherent mistakes become more apparent. The continual complaining is in order to gain something quite intelligible, but loses for him what it is intended to gain.

This same dynamic is frequently operative in marriages, in which each person fails to appreciate what the other is contributing and complains instead about what he is not getting. It is easy to suggest that each should be more appreciative and complimentary, but the good sense of the suggestion is too frequently ignored. Each spouse is making a case that the other owes him something more, and to appreciate the other is to ruin the case. Anyway, one who is mad at someone does not want to make him feel better by appreciating the things that person gives. In clarifying the sense it makes to not appreciate the other, we bring forth critical issues and from there attempt to resolve them so that each can appreciate the other without feeling that by so doing he is losing ground.

Any action occurs in a framework of multiple considerations and complex social competencies. Considerable which is right and good may be involved even in misunderstandings and in inappropriate actions. Most important, we fully understand the source of the errors only as we locate them in the context of everything else that the client is doing which does make sense: the errors make sense themselves only in the context of the ways the client makes sense. In the case just discussed, the husband's obvious error in misjudging his wife's contributions makes sense only in the context of what he is trying to accomplish through his argument and the reasons he has for doing so. To fail to understand the sense behind the mistake is to leave ourselves with too few options for effective interventions.

When you want to change someone's mind, it seems only natural to explain how the other is mistaken: show how he is wrong so that he can see the errors and correct them. Emphasizing instead the ways the person makes sense runs contrary to a deeply ingrained everyday tendency, for most people feel that to emphasize the good sense involved in someone's mistaken views is to strengthen those views and weaken their own counterargument. It is unusual indeed in everyday conversation to see anyone legitimize someone else's views and then use that as a basis to challenge the mistakes. Legitimizing may require considerable study and practice because it is sometimes complex and because it runs so counter to deeply ingrained everyday tendencies. It takes some getting used to.

Consider as an everyday case a parent whose daughter has gotten into trouble for talking in class. She says that one of her classmates asked her about a problem, and she was just answering him when the teacher yelled at her for talking: it all seems so terribly unfair. The inclinations of most parents either would be sympathetic with the daughter and in opposition to the teacher, who it seems should be more understanding, or would be sympathetic with the classroom authority and in opposition to the daughter, who should learn to conduct herself more appropriately in a classroom. Either position has its

problems. Siding against the teacher supports the daughter but fails to resolve the classroom problem, for more trouble awaits the youngster who continues to talk in class. But by siding with the teacher, the parent comes across to the youngster as insensitive, callous, and not to be trusted; the chances are that the youngster will not listen and the problem will continue.

The issue is problematic only when one sees it as a choice between supporting the youngster and requiring her to change; it makes good sense to do both. The best solution is to legitimize the youngster's position and show her the sense that she makes, and from there to recommend or even require

92

alternatives. One might begin by saying, "It does seem unfair, because you were just answering a question and you did not mean to be causing trouble. When someone asks you something it is really hard to know what to do. Should you just ignore him (but that doesn't seem right because he is your friend) or should you answer him (but then the teacher is going to get mad)? I can see how it's a real problem. Anyway, when the teacher yells at you that makes it hard to want to do anything to please her." One is in a better position after that work out a solution and expect some compliance: "It may not seem quite fair, but you still have to get along there. Could you talk to your friend before class and tell him that you are not going to answer his questions because you cannot afford to get into any more trouble?" There is no need to choose between being sympathetic and understanding as opposed to being challenging and directive. Sequence the responses, and there is ample room to do both.

Legitimizing accredits the client as one who makes sense, for by showing time and again that one view after another and one action after another make sense, we show that the client herself makes sense and we make the case airtight. Indeed, within the context of the therapeutic relationship, everything the client does is considered to make some sense, even prior to our understanding the sense that it actually makes. The client is simply ineligible to not make sense, for there is nothing he does or could possibly do which we would see as making no sense at all.

Consider a young woman who accepted a ride from a stranger, sensing full well she was inviting trouble, and barely slipped away from him without being physically harmed. She is puzzled by her action and sees no reason why she might have done it: she considers herself not merely unwise but entirely irrational as well. Our initial comments should affirm that she, like other persons, acts on reasons. Beginning with "that is puzzling" confirms the good sense the woman has in realizing that something is quite amiss. From there, we might go on: "I don't know what your reasons were for what you did, but surely you had some reasons. You are not the sort of person who would do something for just no reason at all." Perhaps further inquiry might reveal that the young woman has been bound by stifling moral conventions in which any affections at all were considered improper and indecent. In accepting the ride, she was rebelling against the constrictions of her upbringing, although in a manner that ensured she would find few pleasures and would receive her just punishment for it. She accepted the ride then in order to slip outside her moral conventions without abandoning them altogether.

The "you are not the sort of person who would do something for just no reason at all" statement accredits the woman, for-despite her puzzling behavior-she is held to make sense in the same general ways that everyone else makes sense. The comment is an easy move, for it requires only that we understand our common language concept of persons: persons may or may not be conscious of the reasons they have, but to be a person is to be the sort of being which has reasons on which he acts. No person is the sort of being which does things for just no reason at all. While obvious, the move is also essential. It introduces making sense as a logical requisite for any action and so invites us to find the reasons the woman has, to make sense of them for her, and from there, to help her to reevaluate them. In this way, our clients are simply ineligible to make no sense, for the logic of our common language concepts requires that there be some sense to anything they do.

Legitimizing might involve the use of any of the common language concepts. Generally, to legitimize the observation or action, we might mention the reasons a person has and then use situations, individual characteristics, or past experiences by which these characteristics were acquired.

Legitimizing interpretations are generally non-pejorative and often quite sympathetic, and so are readily accepted by the client. Because they convey the inherent sensibleness in the client's position, they come across as quite empathic-often more empathic than active listening statements which merely rephrase the client's statements and feelings. By legitimizing we show that we really understand the complexities of what is involved.

Legitimizing contrasts most obviously with standard rational-

emotive interventions, in which Ellis argues to his clients that their views and beliefs are irrational. In sharp contrast, we show our clients that their views and actions make sense— indeed often more sense than they ever considered they might make. In so doing, we accredit the person as rational and sensible.

Clients are often puzzled by their actions and see themselves as making little sense or being generally irrational. One who sees himself as irrational has little reason to attempt to apply his irrationality to solve his own problems, for he is rational enough to see that can see that the application of further irrationality is no way out. By legitimizing, we challenge our clients' views of themselves as irrational and show the inherent sensibleness in even the most puzzling of actions. By so doing, we instill in our clients some confidence that they make sense and legitimate expectations that they can profitably apply their good sense to solve their problems. Support for legitimizing is given by attitude change research which indicates that when we thoroughly and adequately address the rationales supporting the client's initial positions we markedly increase our therapeutic influence.[48]

Many theories of psychopathology ignore altogether the fabric of human sensibleness and begin instead with mechanistic interpretations or with irrationalities. Psychoanalytic and psychodynamic traditions see man as irrational; behaviorism holds that one's so-called reasons for actions are unimportant in understanding human behavior. Humanistic traditions challenge these mechanistic concepts but do not elaborate adequately the alternatives; client-centered therapists avoid any evaluation whatsoever of their clients. Gestaltists, who also avoid evaluation in their sessions, nonetheless emphasize in their theories the irrationality of human perception. Rational-emotive therapists emphasize the irrationality of troublesome views and begin interventions with strong argument to the client that his views are irrational. The under-emphasis of the ordinary sensibleness of problematic actions may be due to the everyday tactic of beginning with what is wrong and also to the tendency in social sciences theorizing to sideline commonsense explanations in favor of the theoretical alternatives. Much of the good work on the fabric of everyday human reasoning is left to the fields of philosophy and logic.[49]

While prevailing theories underemphasize ordinary human sensibleness, it should not be assumed automatically that those who identify with these theories fail similarly to take into account the sensibleness of their clients. Practitioners from most orientations show something of the sensibleness of their clients' experiences and actions. But legitimizing can be carried much further than is commonly done, for we can do it more frequently and can increase the impact by using terms that the clients themselves are familiar with and can intuitively understand. "Legitimize" was suggested by Ossorio as a general policy for therapeutic influence and stands here as one of the most salient characteristics of the current psychotherapy approach.

By showing the ways our clients make sense already, we gain a considerable advantage. Excuse the wordplay, but we can expect to do considerably better with our rational clients than others do with their irrational clients.

Make it acceptable

Troubled persons conclude too readily that whatever is wrong is unacceptable, intolerable, and inexcusable, and is to be condemned, concealed, rejected, and squashed out of existence. Even the most commonplace mistakes and failures may be taken as evidence of intolerable inadequacy. This indicates a broad-ranging inability to accept the weaknesses and limitations of life as a fallible human being.

Too frequently, the client holds that she is absolutely unacceptable as she is and that she must change before she or anyone else can tolerate her. The task as she sees it is to take an inexcusably inadequate individual and alter her enough to change her into an acceptable human being. We must avoid any implicit agreement with this formulation, for it is a sure invitation to failure. One might be brilliant and nonetheless make only minimal headway in changing an unacceptable failure into an acceptable human being.

We do well to begin instead with a reformulation of the problem. Our essential therapeutic position here is that the client is in important ways already acceptable but is unable to see himself that way. The issue then is no longer one of making an unacceptable wretch into an acceptable human being. The issue rather is one of convincing the client that he is already acceptable, and of beginning there in understanding and changing troublesome characteristics.

A client who sees that his therapist places the best light on whatever characteristics of his are revealed comes to expect that other sensitive

issues will be similarly understood and interpreted in a favorable manner. Making personal characteristics acceptable thus tends to improve the therapeutic relationship and to further open the channels of communication.

Clients often feel that by accepting their troublesome characteristics, they would resign themselves to them, whereas by condemning and rejecting these characteristics, they can expect to make them vanish. Generally, it works just the other way around, for by rejecting troublesome aspects of themselves, people merely lose conscious awareness of the nature of those problems, and leave themselves in no position to puzzle things through and to generate alternatives. The gentle tolerance of existing foibles and failings is not a resignation to continuing the problems, but rather a first step in generating alternative solutions. Sometimes it is useful to explain this directly: "As we look at these things, you condemn yourself so harshly and make yourself so uncomfortable that you are going to force yourself to forget all about them as soon as you can. To remain conscious of these factors you must be gentle with yourself when you see them, so that you can keep them comfortably in mind and work with them."

We make things acceptable by creating an atmosphere of comfortableness and acceptance, and by presenting things in ways that the client can most readily accept. We should structure the interview so that it is as comfortable as possible for the client. The individual entering therapy has been unable to manage well on his own, and oftentimes is troubled and embarrassed by his lack of independence and self-sufficiency. In many cases, he is unsettled also by the expected un-savoriness of whatever might be revealed about himself: he is sure that the therapist sees through him and that his multitude of sins, embarrassments, inadequacies, and failures will be exposed. Such an individual might be set at ease by restructuring the relationship in the following manner: "It sounds as though you feel I am here to evaluate you. Some concern is understandable, of course, for everyone has some initial apprehension about what is going to happen. You are forgetting, however, that you are the one who is here to evaluate me. You use the first session to see if I am someone whom you are comfortable talking to, and who can understand you, be supportive, and offer you some constructive thoughts and suggestions. If I meet your requirements, then you continue with me. If I do not meet your requirements, then you seek somebody else. So I am the one who is being evaluated, and you are the one who is doing the evaluating. You need to keep that in mind here in our first interview."

We thus reinterpret and restructure the relationship to make being in the position of a client more acceptable. The reinterpretation reaffirms the right of the client to choose his therapist, and thus eases somewhat the problems of unequal status between client and therapist. Usually it lessens the tensions and invites the client to continue in the relationship on a more equal footing.

Be comfortable: A client naturally gauges the acceptability of what he reveals from the responses he receives from the therapist. The comfortableness of the therapist is a critical indicator for the client of whether the issues are tolerably comfortable or socially uncomfortable and inappropriate. Continuing warmth and acceptance suggest that the client is quite acceptable already and thereby invite the client to see himself in a similar manner. He counts as acceptable, at least to this one important person. Thus, it is essential that we maintain an easy comfortableness and set our clients similarly at ease.

Use humor: Humor is extremely important. A message which is otherwise ignored or resisted may be more easily accepted when stated in a humorous manner. One woman, for instance, is married to a chronic alcoholic, but ignores the realities and clings tenaciously to her wishful fantasies. "If only he would stop drinking," she argues again for the fifteenth time this session, "then I'm sure together we could work out the rest of the problems." The therapist has been trying throughout the session to challenge the "if only" reasoning but has failed even to get her attention, and she continues persistently' Some humor in the challenge might turn the trick: "Exactly, we might begin "and if frogs had wings then they wouldn't bump their asses." This breaks the tension and allows her a moment off the drivenness of her argument.

Humor adds sparkle and intrigue, and allows one to enjoy issues which would otherwise appear mundane or ugly. Humor thus is one way of making existing problems and foibles at least minimally acceptable. A sense of humor cannot be introduced artificially, for one must genuinely appreciate what is intriguing and enjoyable about a situation so that it comes across as natural and supportive. Sessions which are effective are often characterized by a strong note of enjoyment and humor between therapist and client. The message is that there is something worthwhile and appealing in even the dreariest of circumstances.

The introduction of humor is foreign to many therapist trainees, who are understandably concerned with showing respect, not offending their clients, and avoiding making errors in the sessions. Some precautions might be noted, of course, for humor relies on social relationship and context, and an attempt at levity inappropriate to the relationship is simply not funny. But training programs which stress so strongly the seriousness of psychotherapy and fail to mention the enjoyment and humor do everyone a disservice. Sessions without humor can be dreary indeed and too familiar for clients who already take themselves far too seriously anyway. We should establish a respectful relationship, then introduce humor, and use the clients' responses to gauge its appropriateness and effect. Humor, successfully introduced, can go a long way to challenge and alter the drab and humorless views many clients have of themselves and of their lives.

Select acceptable phrasing: The phrasing of an interpretation may make an essential idea more or less acceptable. We should phrase interpretations so that the essential ideas are conveyed in a manner least offensive and most acceptable to a particular client. Consider the following interpretations of a husband's continuing hostile and antagonistic actions:

1. "You are trying to get even with your wife for the way she is mistreating you."

2. "You are trying to show your wife that she cannot get away with mistreating you that way."

The first interpretation may evoke considerable resistance, for one would not want to accept that his motive is retaliation and vengeance. The second interpretation is considerably more acceptable, for one will easily agree that he should not allow someone who mistreats him to continue getting away with it. The two interpretations are alternate descriptions of what is in many ways the same essential motivation. The interpretation which is most acceptable invites the client to accept and understand the issues. We go from there to reevaluate the issues and to consider alternate courses of action.

Emphasize positives: One who fails or wrongs others in spite of his good intentions may indulge in self-recrimination for his failure, and can miss or ignore entirely the importance of his good intentions. We may make such incidents more acceptable by introducing and emphasizing the importance of the intentions: "You see only the failure. Your intentions, however, were good ones, and you are missing entirely the importance of what you were attempting to accomplish. You see only the outcome which follows your actions and are absolutely blind to what you yourself are contributing. What you contribute is the attempt to make things go well, although the resulting outcome is not always in your control. You need to be more aware of your own contributions to your actions." The individual who emphasizes failure is shown here that his is a failure to see and understand his own good intentions. The recognition of good intention is generally comforting, for it enables one to accept more easily one's own actions in the face of uncertain outcomes. Emphasizing the positives creates a supportive atmosphere and makes it easier to accept other interpretations which are challenging or otherwise uncomfortable.

Underplay negatives: We may underplay the strength of a portrayal to make it more palatable. Suppose we suggest to a client that he was angry, and he feels that this casts him in a poor light and so objects to the interpretation. To underplay, we comment: "I'm not saying that you were really angry but perhaps just slightly angry-as anyone would have been." The milder interpretation would be easier for the client to accept, and the underinterpretation is all we really need anyway, for once the client acknowledges that he was angry at all then we can discuss the causes of the anger and how to rechannel it. We need only a foothold, and the acceptance of any anger provides an entryway.

Introduce norms: Persons too often see their own inadequacies as extraordinary and fail to see that others too have similar problems. Information about others' experiences in similar situations may invite the client to alter unrealistically high standards and expectations, and to accept otherwise unacceptable aspects of himself. An individual going through separation and divorce may find himself confused and frazzled much of the time, and worry that in addition to failing at a marriage he is now on the verge of losing his sanity. Anxiety and embarrassment about his emotional instability further complicate an

already difficult condition. Some basic information about what is generally experienced by others in such situations should give him a better sense that such experiences are normal and expectable, and would enable him to tolerate better the painful process of separation. Uncomfortable and unstabilizing emotions are the normal course in divorce experiences, and one who understands that is in a better position to accept and to struggle through the experience.

Comparisons to others and a lowering of unrealistically high standards may be some of the major benefits of sensitivity and personal growth groups, in which participants often mention relief in finding out that others have problems too; they become more comfortable with the vagaries and imperfectibility of human nature.

When we do present unfavorable interpretations, we should present them as possibilities or as completions of an otherwise favorable picture. We should avoid unfavorable character assessments as primary accounts of personal difficulties.

It is not necessarily sufficient for a therapist to merely accept what the client says. A therapist who avoids condemning but expresses no opinions invites uncomfortable suspicions about where he really stands and inadvertently may even convey agreement with the client's own self-condemning attitudes. One who intervenes actively makes it clear where he stands, and encourages confidence and trust in his position. Therefore, we must be more than merely accepting in order to promote greater self-acceptance in our clients.

In a friendly manner, we may interpret, challenge, banter, and even humor a client to a more self-accepting attitude. Consider the client who is giving exaggerated importance to relatively minor transgressions and is squirming under the weight of his own self-recrimination. Merely accepting the self-recriminative statements would do little to encourage self-acceptance and might convey implicit agreement with the acid of his comments. Some alternative is needed. We might playfully exaggerate and dramatize the client's position: "Sounds like `what a great sinner I am.' You're saying, `My sins are not the sins of ordinary mortals, but are exceptional, grand, extravagant, unique, and tremendously important sins.'" The effect here is to jostle the client out of his self-indulgence and to make the case forcefully that he himself is the agent ascribing exaggerated importance to his own relatively minor misdemeanors. The intervention is a good-natured
challenge to the client's position, and it invites him to accept his own transgressions as relatively minor.

Thus, we encourage the client to accept things by being comfortable with them ourselves, by presenting them in a supportive manner, and also by challenging directly the client's tendencies to condemn and reject himself. Analysis of and challenge to the client's self-critical tendencies are dealt with more thoroughly in chapter 10 on self-critical tendencies.

Some contend that merely talking about feelings and concerns in a supportive atmosphere leads to greater self-acceptance and to therapeutic improvement. It does sometimes, but oftentimes it does not. We should ask whether these issues are all that unacceptable to begin with and whether the client has concealed these concerns previously or talks about them freely. Concerns that are frightening secrets might become more acceptable just by being brought out in the open. Someone who had been sexually molested or had an illegal abortion, and was then required to remain silent, would stand to profit greatly from talking the experience through in a supportive atmosphere. Revealing such secrets and having them accepted make them more personally acceptable, and can be extremely therapeutic. In major personal losses, expressing grief is especially important in helping to accept the loss. In contrast, other concerns are not particularly unacceptable to begin with and have been talked about too much already. For instance, a woman who complains about her neglectful child or alcoholic husband to anyone who will listen will not profit from merely going through the same dreary story again and again in a supportive atmosphere. The concerns have been thoroughly covered, and now need to be reinterpreted and challenged.

Good interventions are those which deal with significant issues in a manner which encourages comfortableness and which involves and intrigues the client. "Make it acceptable" sets a standard for therapeutic interventions and for the nature of a therapeutic experience. Interpretations should assist the client in understanding issues in a way which encourages acceptance and appreciation of oneself. An overall effect of a therapeutic session should be an awareness that one is acceptable already; from there, further possibilities are available for making life better. In general, a client should leave the sessions feeling better because of the therapeutic experience. While we are not able to achieve this in every session with every client, it is nonetheless an important objective. When too many clients leave their sessions more confused, unsure, troubled, or miserable with themselves, it indicates that insufficient attention is being paid to making the experience an acceptable one.

It is wrong to use the amount of uncomfortableness generated by an interpretation as an indication of the depth or significance of the interpretation. Sometimes some interpretations do hurt, but we do not argue that they should hurt and we should not use the number of tears or the amount of pain in a session to gauge the quality of the therapeutic experience.

Encouraging the client to better accept himself is an important objective of perhaps a majority of psychotherapies, but the means used to encourage self-acceptance vary considerably from orientation to orientation. Psychoanalytic and psychodynamic emphasize timing as the way to make interpretations acceptable. Client-centered holds that being warm, real, and empathic enables the client to accept what he shares of himself. Transactional analysis uses picturesque terms and stories to make its interpretations fun. Behavior therapy makes things acceptable by attributing problems not to personal choices but to conditioned response patterns, and in systematic desensitization by giving soothing suggestions to relax and then presenting the tough stuff a little bit at a time. Cognitive behavioral teaches control of pejorative statements about oneself. Rational-emotive argues that to not accept oneself is irrational. "Reframing," popularized by Milton Erickson and Jay Haley, and widely used in communications and family systems approaches, involves redescribing, relabeling, or reinterpreting an action, usually to make it more acceptable to the client. The "positive connotation" technique in other family therapies is similar. Note the contrast between client-centered counseling, which seeks to promote self-acceptance by accepting everything the client says, and rational-emotive therapy, which seeks the same objective by challenging forcefully the client's beliefs that he is unacceptable.

Confirm the client's control

An automobile rental company advertises, "Let us put you in the driver's seat." If we were to attempt that strategy with our clients, some would step compliantly into the driver's seat only to step out again when conditions got rough or when it suited them to abandon

the journey, and others would not want the responsibility of being in control of their lives in the first place. Our strategy instead is to show the client that he is now, has always been, and always will be in the driver's seat. Once one acknowledges that he exercises control anyway and resigns himself to it, then he goes on from there to learn to control things more advantageously and so get where he wants to go with fewer accidents. We might use the image of being already in the driver's seat to convey to clients that our task as therapists is not to talk them into taking control of their lives, but rather, since they are in control already, to confirm it for them and from there to look at ways to control things to suit them better.

There are ways in which one is a passenger in his life, and ways also in which one is contributing to and controlling the course of that life. We do well to begin by emphasizing the control the person is exerting and from there to fill in the picture with the ways he does not have control. We must confirm the ways in which the client is not undirected, but misdirected; not weak, but inept in how he is using his strengths; not adrift in life, but paddling crosswise and backwards against the current.

When a person cannot seem to decide something, we could see this as an inadequacy or weakness, which it is, and we could also see it as a way the person has of controlling things by not deciding, and thus as something more than mere inadequacy. As an example, take the perhaps too familiar situation of a man (it could as well be a woman) who is married and having an affair, and who worries about it continually but cannot seem to decide whether to leave home or to terminate the affair. The failure to decide can be seen as an inadequacy on his part, for it is causing considerable turmoil and pain for himself and everyone else involved, but it is more than just a failure to make up his mind. Quite probably, the man has fears both of leaving his wife and of losing his lover, and fears also that either choice he makes may be the wrong one. Thus, he has reasons for not deciding, for by not deciding he avoids making the wrong choice and he also keeps both women. Without acknowledging it to himself, he is acting on these quite intelligible reasons, so he is genuinely in control of his own apparent confusion in the matter.

To convince the client that he is in control, we must do more than merely state that he is in control. The best way to confirm for the client that he is controlling things is to make explicit the reasons he has for

the control he exercises and then if necessary to legitimize those reasons. In this case, we could mention that there are ways to go wrong with either choice and that since he fears making the wrong decision, he stays clear by making no decision at all. To legitimize those fears, we could mention the pressures he feels from his wife and family and from his lover as well, the advantages of each, and the pain there would be in losing either woman.

He seeks safety by avoiding the wrong decision, but there may also be real satisfactions from being involved with two women. We could mention such satisfactions in order to complete the picture and suggest that since he gains something from each and the attention is flattering, he has that further reason not to give it up. Interpretation of his fears of making the wrong decision is the more sympathetic of these, but interpretation of the satisfactions involved in having both worlds completes the picture, for it includes the ways his own appetites contribute to his problems. The thrust changes then from "Are you able to decide?" to "Are you willing to give up those satisfactions?" Both interpretations are accurate enough, and both have their place in our pragmatic approach.

Making explicit his reasons for not deciding spoils the innocence of his acting on those reasons without responsibility for the actions. By bringing to consciousness his reasons for not deciding, we force him either to continue to act on those reasons, but now consciously and by choice, or to reassess his reasons and do something else. He must then either choose between the two women or choose not to choose, but either way he is shown to be in charge.

By emphasizing the ways the client controls things, we may even recast apparent failures into modest successes. Some clients are attempting to achieve particular objectives that are intelligible enough but too easily missed in the light of other obvious and more socially important objectives at which they are failing. In such cases, we do well to emphasize the individual objectives which are sought after and successfully attained.

One young man has a history of job failures, and ambivalent attitudes toward his parents who are themselves quite successful and who expect from him nothing less than outstanding achievements. The young man comments: "I cannot even hold a job. My parents put a lot of pressure on me and are always after me to accomplish something, but nothing does any good. I guess I am just a big failure."

Our therapeutic response is to recast the failure as follows: "It strikes me that not holding a job in the face of that sort of pressure is more than merely failing to hold a job. We would better describe it as refusing to be pressured into something, as holding your own against the pressure. You are not the sort of person who buckles under pressure, and you have been holding your own with your folks, and quite successfully."

At doing something socially or personally acceptable he is a failure, but in resisting parental pressure-which to this individual is paramount-he is a modest success. Were a therapist to begin instead with the failure, he would be accepting at face value the proclaimed inadequacy and would have a poor foundation indeed for further interventions. How much time might be spent trying to convince the fellow to get up on time instead of sleeping through the alarm, and just how much could one expect to accomplish anyway with a young man who is so thoroughly inadequate that he cannot even make it to work on time? But by beginning with the success, we are in an excellent position for further interventions. The young man has reasons for resisting parental pressure, and through an understanding of these reasons, we can help him to reevaluate and find other less costly ways to hold his own and exert his independence. Perhaps he complies overtly with his parents while resisting covertly, and encouragement toward overt independence would affirm his self-respect and free him from such costly passive ways of resistance. Perhaps we could interpret his having to resist as itself an indication that he lacks real freedom and, to the extent that he values independence, encourage him to break away and chart his own course. The beginning interpretation of the ways the client controls and is successful opens these and other strategies for practical interventions.

In the two cases just discussed, showing the reasons for the actions is a basic method of confirming to the client that he is controlling those actions. Showing the sense the actions make supports the argument that he is actually making those actions. As a general principle: showing the reasons for the behavior and legitimizing serve as a solid foundation for confirming to the client that he is indeed in control of that behavior. By confirming the ways the client is successful, we construct again the familiar therapeutic double bind: should the client continue in the same manner to resist his parents, then he is acting on

intelligible reasons and being successful; should he discontinue the pattern, then he is cured.

One might say that the young man is succeeding at being a failure, which is not incorrect but is so abbreviated as to miss the essentials entirely. What the young man is succeeding at is resisting his parents, and being a failure is merely the way he goes about it and the price he has to pay. Failure is the means to success and the price of that success, but it is not of itself success.

We confirm that the client is in control by interpreting the ways he takes control and also, importantly, by treating him as someone who is in control. Merely telling someone repeatedly that he is in control of his life belies the argument, for one who is in control is most certainly in control also of whether he is going to see it that way. It would be more consistent to mention that he is in control, and from there to point out that he has the choice of whether or not to see it that way, and then to support the point by showing the reasons he has to avoid acknowledging his contributions. Similarly, reassuring someone repeatedly that he can do something is a way of treating him as someone badly in need of reassurance, just as avoiding challenging someone when it is called for is a way of treating him as fragile or too easily thrown off course by a challenge. Too much reassurance can come across as patronizing. The message is "You are weak, but with my continued reassurance you can make it anyway." Indeed, we may do better instead with constructive challenge, for that is a way of treating our clients as persons who are sturdy enough to take it.

While interpretations and challenges should be constructed to be as readily acceptable as possible, some issues are particularly sensitive and some clients particularly touchy, so that with some interpretations we lose ground and find the client upset and angry that we would say what we did. Should the interpretation be a poor one we are free to withdraw it, but what about an interpretation which is as gentle as we can make it and really important? The client may be controlling the conversation through his anger and upset, and a good move here is to confirm that control: "By becoming so upset and angry over my comment, you give me the message that I am upsetting you and that I better not say those things any more or I might be responsible for causing you real harm. By becoming upset, you effectively stonewall my comments and prevent me from saying those things it seems I should not be saying." We could go on with the original interpretation at this point if the client permits it, or we could withdraw it if necessary or water it down to something more acceptable. In any case, we confirm that the client is strong enough to exercise control over what he permits us to say. We thus interpret the control that he is exercising and also treat him as someone who has the control that he does indeed have. Being treated as in control gives him that status in the therapeutic relationship, and is one important step in his seeing himself as in control and beginning to use it more suitably.

Along these same lines, Gestaltists change "I can't" statements to "I won't" statements to stress oppositional motivations, and game interpretations in transactional analysis stress the control and resulting satisfactions in apparent weaknesses. Ossorio suggests as a therapeutic policy that we choose anger over fear interpretations, for anger interpretations implicate the force and control the client is exercising while fear interpretations convey the weakness. Analytic and dynamic orientations interpret anger and resistance motivations in apparent weaknesses. But some orientations are weak in this area, notably the behavioral orientations, which focus too exclusively on how one is controlled by situations and by past learning, and overlook the subtleties of how one is in control already.

Go beyond victim senarios

Appearing persecuted and victimized might seem at first glance bereft of real satisfactions, yet persons do cast themselves as victims by choice and for a variety of basically intelligible reasons. Persons may cast themselves as victims in order to appear noble and gain support, to avoid responsibility themselves, or to cast others as ignoble persecutors and oppressors, thereby making others responsible. A person might have one such reason or several in combination together.

Challenging victim philosophies is complementary to confirming the clients' control. By recognizing that they actively cast themselves as victims and by legitimizing the reasons they have for doing so, we accredit our clients as contributors and participants rather than mere victims in their lives, and so confirm the control that they do have.

Acknowledging the clients' contribution to victim acts affirms their control in their scenarios, but it also ruins their acts as victims and is thus one of the touchiest of interventions to bring off successfully. The exploration of victim acts is as essential as it is complex and sensitive, for the client must see the contributions he can and does make to his condition so that he might be in a position to redirect his contributions to better uses. We must interpret and legitimize the reasons

111

clients have for presenting themselves as victims, and only from there attempt to challenge the acts.

In many relationships, the one who hurts the most gains all the attention and concern, and others who are doing well are always responsible. These folks accept as fundamental the ideology that the one who is the most miserable therefore merits our concern the most-an ideology that has been termed "victimism" for its unfaltering faith in the goodness of the apparent victim regardless of the causes of his or her sorry state. The contributions of misconceived views of Christian suffering have been explored elsewhere.[50] When someone casts himself as a victim to involve others, we should interpret the advantages of being the sufferer, challenge the ideology, and invite the person involved to try other ways of gaining concern and managing responsibilities.

One may cast himself as a victim in order to avoid responsibility for many aspects of his life. Some see power itself and those who exercise power as oppressive, hurtful, and wrong, regardless of the uses of the power. Lord Acton stated as a political maxim that "Power tends to corrupt, and absolute power corrupts absolutely." In essential agreement and applying it to their own lives, these persons squelch their own personal power in order to maintain their innocence and to avoid being corrupt. For apparently ethical reasons they avoid power, and accept and cherish positions of powerlessness, from which they find themselves angry victims of others who wield power.

The misconception here is that oppression belongs exclusively to those in positions of overt power. That may be mainly so in economics and in politics, but in close interpersonal relationships it does not hold at all. One may be every bit as much the oppressor from an inferior position as from an apparently superior one, for the apparently weaker position justifies and camouflages the retaliatory manipulations toward the apparent persecutors. Those who seem strong are held accountable for their actions, whereas

112

those who seem weak are ignored or excused. If you think power corrupts, try powerlessness!

One may cast himself as a victim in order to cast others as the callous perpetrators of the problems, and thus to condemn and punish others for their misconduct, and to pressure them to change. The

"sons of bitches" have made his life miserable, and he is going to hold them fully accountable. There are no incentives here for solving one's own problems, and there is at least one major reason for not solving them: one can blame others only so long as things remain miserable, but were one to show chat he himself could make things improve, he would ruin his case against those culprits who he contends are responsible for his miserable condition.

Some people are indeed victims, for they have been mistreated and abused in various ways throughout their lives: there are neglected childhoods, alcoholic husbands, nagging wives, meddling in-laws, ungrateful children, financial problems, and so on. Many people are also victims of their own misconceptions and maladaptive tendencies. But there are very few people who are merely victims, for they are also participants in the lives they live, and their choices and actions do contribute for better or worse to their fortunes and misfortunes. Victim acts cast one as merely a victim and not a participant. Our task in challenging the act is to emphasize the manner in which the person is also a participant, and so to encourage him to understand and redirect the nature of his own participation.

One who is running a victim act is not interested in solving the hardships or even in making the best of those that cannot be changed. Rather, the interest is in what he might gain through being the victim, and any real effort to change things or to make the best of things would ruin the course of action.

Claims to being a victim may be true enough as far as they go, for life can be harsh and oppression real. We might try to sort through how much of the problems result from genuine oppression and how much from manageable hardships and maladaptive inclinations, but such questions become too readily confounded and unresolvable. Those who are mistreated also mistreat others in turn, and each contributes to the overall problems of the others. It is better to focus on the pragmatic or "in order to" aspects of the argument: What is the client attempting to gain by investing in his claims to being a victim, and what sorts of outcomes are to be expected? We can even agree that one has been treated unfairly in particular ways and still make a case for not pursuing the claim against those who have no interest in listening.

A young adult who was neglected or mistreated by his parents might feel quite reasonably that they owe him more than they gave him, and

argue continually that he was wronged in order to convince them and make them give him the love and consideration which is his right. We can agree that he does have a case, for children should be treated better than that, and then from there use the concept of a bad debt to show how he is investing his energies and wasting his life in something that is quite clearly uncollectable. "Your parents really did not give you what they should have when you were growing up, and it is quite understandable that you feel they messed up your life and that they ought to make up for it now. But it is a bad debt, for there appears to be no way to collect it. You argue that they owe it to you, and that they ought to recognize your rights and be more considerate of your feelings. But in doing so you merely waste your time and mess yourself up. It is like driving across town every day to collect from somebody who owes you some money, finding every time that the person doesn't have it to give to you, and then doing the same thing the next day. You get insulted and angry all over again each time; you waste your time and deplete your energy. It is better to write off the bad debt and go on with your life. That is what you need to do with you parents: they ignore you and get angry when you expect things from them, for they see you as accusing them and have no interest in listening."

In agreeing that others are not living up to their responsibilities, we come across as supportive and sympathetic, and from our position there as supporters and allies, we can more easily challenge the client to write off the bad debt. We hold him not entirely accountable for his problems, but then point out how his current attitudes contribute to and maintain these problems, and show him how to make changes.

We identify problems as victim acts by an exaggerated miserableness in the face of rather everyday hardships, by a staunch commitment to arguing the victim position, and by an unwillingness to accept alternative solutions. These persons must relinquish their commitments to being victims before they have any real interest in considering alternative solutions.

Social conventions are more understanding and sympathetic to women who are oppressed by men than to men who are oppressed by women, and thus offer more opportunities for women to benefit by casting themselves as the abused or neglected victims of their lovers or spouses. A woman who contends that the bastard she is involved with is ruining her life gains sympathy and support, and turns her friends against her oppressor. In contrast, most men avoid casting themselves overtly as oppressed and victimized by women, for men strive to see themselves as strong and superior, and they feel humiliated rather than supported when abused or abandoned by women. While there is more support for women who present themselves as victimized by their men, there is little real long term benefit for either men or women in casting themselves as victims. We benefit persons of either sex by challenging the acts.

In challenging victim acts we attempt to take away something that may be a cornerstone for a person's whole way of life, and because of this we should be prepared for quite a contest. Several tactics make the message easier to swallow, including legitimizing the reasons the client has for the act, making our interpretations acceptable by acknowledging that others do the same things, avoiding generating resistance by accepting the justifications the client offers, and so on. To make the challenge work, we must also offer something better as a replacement. A woman who has invested so much in blaming others might be complimented on how well she has managed nonetheless, and asked to consider all the energy she has invested in holding others responsible and to imagine how remarkably well she might do were she to use that energy to her own benefit. The message must be one of optimism, confirming existing strengths and indicating a better life ahead as those strengths are put to better use.

Victim acts might easily be termed manipulations or games, but since these labels appear pejorative there is practical reason to avoid using them with our clients. Our task is to describe the nature of what the person is doing, and to legitimize and make sense of it: we should avoid using general category descriptions which indicate that the actions are inauthentic or wrong without indicating exactly what is going on. Thus, we might state that the client is acting to hold others responsible and legitimize his reasons for doing that, but we avoid the pejorative connotation of manipulation or playing games.

We should watch out whenever we find ourselves feeling sorry for our clients. In general, we feel sorry for others when we have no therapeutic plan of action, and so see only the hopelessness and pain. In contrast, when we are actively engaged in finding solutions, we do not dwell on feeling sorry for someone but invest in the promise for change: we are too involved with what we are attempting to contribute. Feelings of sorrow and pity for someone convey that the situation is hopeless, and may even encourage a client in his own in-dulgence in misery and self-pity. Feeling sorry for oneself is a primary aspect of a victim position and need not be encouraged by a complementary position on the part of the therapist. Compassion for our clients is important, but sorrow or pity indicates that we have been taken in by victim acts and that we have too few ideas for therapeutic interventions.

Most therapeutic orientations are wary of victim acts. Transactional analysis uses games interpretations to challenge victim acts by indicating the satisfactions attained through the appearance of being a victim. "Wooden Leg" portrays social lameness as a manipulative self-presentation constructed to avoid responsibilities-after all, what can you expect from a man with a "wooden leg"? When one allows others to take advantage, "Now I've Got You, You Son of a Bitch" (NIGYSOB) portrays it as a ploy to gain the final satisfaction of proving how very much they wronged him. The clever humor makes games interpretations such as these easier to accept. Behavior modification suggests that attention reinforces and thus maintains the complaining, and several orientations-including existential and humanistic-focus on the avoidance of responsibility. "Don't buy victim acts" was introduced by Ossorio as a policy for psychotherapy.

If it works, don't fix it

Special care must be taken to maintain the sometimes subtle distinctions between characteristics which are strengths and those which are failings, in order to continually affirm existing adequacies. "If it works, don't fix it" is a reminder to avoid introducing uncertainties into areas which are functional and to reserve our tinkering for that which is dysfunctional already.

It is too easy, when frustrated by subtle and perplexing issues, to fail to uphold strengths, and to analyze and challenge those more obvious characteristics which seem to conceal the elusive problems. It is better in such cases to acknowledge that problems are not always apparent and to have patience with the investigative process. Problems are most easily seen within the structure of existing strengths, so any failure to uphold strengths serves only to conceal from us the important issues. It is better in such cases to have no answers than to be satisfied with the wrong answers.

Tinkering with strengths is considered a mistake in most orientations, but not in all. An opposing position holds that what appear to be strengths and virtues may instead be covers and defenses against underlying pathologies, and as such impede therapy. Such underlying pathologies are held to have been determined by experiences and conflicts of early childhood, and to be nonetheless of fundamental importance to present character. Long term regressive approaches attempt to strip away present functional characteristics to regress the patient to states which are developmentally earlier and less mature, so that childhood conflicts may be re-experienced, analyzed, and defused of their pathological potential and character may be reintegrated in a healthier manner. Involved here is the peeling away of present adaptive characteristics, in the expectation of being able to reassemble the patient later along healthier lines. The approach is patterned on a surgical analogy: as a surgeon cuts through a healthy abdominal wall to remove an infected appendix, so too should a psychotherapist slice through apparently healthy characteristics to expose and exorcise those otherwise concealed internal pathogens.

Yet once present adaptive strategies are diminished and a regressed state is achieved, is there any guarantee that the patient will be reconstructed in a healthier and more integrated manner? What about the lost opportunities and mishaps which may befall the patient while he is so regressed? Psychotherapy practice sometimes produces detrimental outcomes, and undermining adaptive functioning is one of the ways in which such casualties can occur. Characteristics which are assets, strengths, or virtues should be seen as such and not merely as defenses against underlying pathologies-they should be affirmed rather than undermined. Personal difficulties may be appraised and treated in the presence of such adaptive characteristics, and often all the more easily because of them. Any program to undermine adequacies in order to uncover and treat weaknesses should be undertaken only with the utmost precautions and only after every available alternative has been attempted without progress.

A number of characteristics usually do cushion the emotional impact of stress and adversities, and these are often subject to interpretation as escapes or defenses, perhaps from the infusion of psychoanalytic themes and terminologies. One client, for instance, has a tremendously fast wit, which she uses as a cushion against emotional trauma and also to enjoyably entertain herself and her friends. In the midst of a painful separation and divorce, she questions her adequacy and worth, and her sense of humor is included in the trial by fire: "Oh yeah, I've a great sense of humor, always there with a laugh. It's my way of fooling myself into surviving-old Jannie is easy enough to fool, but a grand lot of good it's doing me." A therapeutic response to this necessarily distinguishes between the source of the difficulties and everything else which is being thrown out to burn: "Be careful! Things go wrong, you're in a squeeze, and your impulse is to question everything about yourself. Something's wrong, granted, but the sense of humor is not a very likely candidate. Your humor enables you to stay involved, to stay alive, even sometimes to sparkle in the midst of the worst. It's a source of stability, an ally-you're taking a cheap shot at your most obvious characteristic. Whatever's going wrong, that's not it, and you had better resign yourself to some serious personal sleuthing."

The same may hold for religious beliefs, commitments to family, or a variety of generally stabilizing social and individual characteristics--any of which might be interpreted as defenses against underlying pathologies. Those characteristics that are generally constructive must be affirmed and not interpreted as obstacles in the search for the underlying pathologies.

7
Assessment

We assess in order to gain the information we need for our therapeutic interventions. The following guidelines are suggestions for gaining practical information:

Assess what matters.
Use ordinary language concepts.
Collaborate.
Learn as you go.
Don't expect the client to be somebody else.

"Assess what matters" is the practical objective, and the following guidelines are the means by which we pursue that objective.

Assess what matters

The objective of assessment is to gain the information we require for most appropriate therapeutic interventions. The information in the assessment must be true rather than false, but its practical utility is most important. It should be self-evident, that all truths are not created equal, nor endowed with inalienable relevance to life, liberty, or the pursuit of happiness. Some information is important or even critical, and other information is tangential or absolutely irrelevant to the conduct of effective psychotherapy. Pragmatics stands as the essential criterion, for the principle standard for adequate assessment is that it contain what is required for the tasks at hand.

Assessment must reveal those factors which contribute to the problems, and also factors which are strengths and might be brought to bear on the problems. Contributing factors might include behaviors, situations, or individual characteristics: most generally there are many identifiable contributing factors, woven together as configurations of behaviors, situations, and individual characteristics.

The *key* factors that we should identify are those which (1) can contribute to major changes in the overall pattern and (2) are most readily altered through something we are in a position to do. These are also called linchpins,[51] as they hold the pattern together. Sullen passivity in the face of obvious provocation would be a key factor with a generally passive client who feels continually taken advantage of: becoming more assertive could change social relationships and break several aspects of the pattern, and we should try to encourage it. Implementing assertiveness in turn might involve changing the individual's concepts, attitudes, motivations, and skills, all of which maintain the passive stance. There can be numerous key factors which might be altered in a case and many other factors which must be altered to change these key factors. Our assessment must identify these key factors as targets for interventions.

Key factors are necessarily present factors, since changes can be made in present factors only. Assessment might cover some past experiences as well, for the past might help to make sense of and legitimize the existing patterns. But the main thrust must be toward those factors which are to be changed and others which are to be used to create the changes, and those are necessarily in the present.

Although psychotherapy is not itself physiological intervention, it falls upon us as counselors and psychotherapists to assess and identify cases in which psychotropic medication or nutritional or other physiological changes would be appropriate, and usually to refer appropriate clients for those treatments. Often, we must also help monitor the effects of medications, to assess whether they continue to be appropriate or whether changes might be called for. So we must also be alert for indications for physiological interventions.

Start with specifics: The most practical focus in any assessment is on key behavioral patterns. We want to know how the persons involved see things, and what they are doing, and what they might do instead which would work out better. The patterns should be given as specifics and not as broad general psychological categorizations. Describing a woman as "continually complaining to justify herself and to hold him responsible" is more useful than describing her as "rigid" or as an "hysterical personality." Describing each of two family members as "using upsetness to show how much he or she cares and to bind the other to him" is more useful than describing them as "fused together" or as an "undifferentiated ego mass." The specifics provide an indispensable basis for therapeutic interventions. Complaining to justify herself is something the woman is actually doing and so might change: we might legitimize and explore her reasons for justifying so much, and from there suggest alternatives. "Rigid" or "hysterical" are global personality categories and not something she is doing-she is not acting in order to be rigid or hysterical. One who focuses on these global categories would not be speaking to anything she might recognize as her own actions and choose to change. Similarly, using upsetness to influence is something that each is doing for understandable reasons and that might be changed; "fused" is something they are but not something they are doing, and it does not suggest practical interventions.

Psychotherapy tries to get persons to change how they see things and what they do and, by affecting these specifics, to promote general changes in personality and social relationships. We must stay with the specifics, for we must tie into these in our attempts to promote changes. Staying with specifics runs contrary to a general trend in our field to underplay simple description and to focus instead on global explanatory formulations.

Omit Extraneous Information. Case analyses too frequently include a clutter of particulars which have no real bearing on the interventions that one might choose. Such extras are padding and have no real business in the assessment, but are included anyway to make the assessment appear thorough or because the assessor was not sure what was important and what was irrelevant, and so included everything to cover his bases. One who is unsure of what is important does not want to omit anything at all and so collects a trash dump of information in which there are a few essentials covered over by everything else. Such extraneous information is not wrong in the sense of inaccurate, but neither is it entirely innocuous. Extraneous information causes problems because it draws attention away from the essentials, and thus confuses and obscures the picture.

Distinguishing between what is essential and what is extraneous may require considerable sensitivity and judgment, but the ability to do so is essential in clinical practice. It is well worth the effort to improve our abilities to make these distinctions.

It is perilous to try to specify categories of information which will invariably be irrelevant, for conceivably even the most tangential information might be relevant somewhere in some circumstances. But some sorts of information are tangential enough to be relevant to few, if any, therapeutic interventions. For instance, a "genogram" assessment, in its focus on the birth order and family lineage of the client and of his mother, father, aunts, uncles, cousins, in-laws, and so on, is going far afield of what matters to the tasks of psychotherapy. Birth order and family lineage are not things that can be changed through psychotherapy, nor are they resources to be used to promote changes. Such information may be interesting, but it is not a key factor for therapeutic intervention.

The case illustrations presented throughout this book give only the information essential to understand the grounds for choosing the suggested interventions. The point of limiting the information given here is not merely to save space: the conciseness is an attempt to give a sense of what an analysis looks like uncluttered with extraneous material, and so to familiarize the reader with this format and perhaps encourage similar conciseness among others.

Most active therapies gear their assessments to what they need to know to intervene, and this is especially so in the behavioral schools. The pragmatic standard for information is an alternative to the principle familiar in liberal arts education that all learning may be important and that concern for its practical utility belongs elsewhere.

Use ordinary language concepts

We use ordinary language concepts to interpret and sometimes reinterpret or translate the client's observations and commentary.

Include Norms Assessment must focus on that which is noteworthy and unique about the case at hand, for that which is human nature or found in all cases can be taken for granted and need not be assessed anew each time. It is those factors which are unique and distinctive that are so essential in tailoring our interventions to the particularities of Joe or Sally.

Our ordinary language concepts are used generally to distinguish the characteristics of one person from another and are well suited to make these distinctions. Ordinary language descriptors portray someone as being a particular way in contrast to other ways which might be expected. When we describe someone as anxious, intelligent, naive, loving, vain-or whatever-we portray him as that way in comparison to how he might have been instead. Someone who is properly described as anxious must be anxious in comparison to others: he might be anxious in comparison to other troubled people, to the average person, to those who are better adapted, to others in stress situations, to others in more ordinary situations, or to other women or other men; he might be more anxious than some or anxious, at least, compared to a yogi who achieves absolute calmness. Points of reference must be stated when they are not implicit from use and context. Descriptions loosed from their points of reference become unmanageably ambiguous. It would be misleading to describe someone as straightforwardly "anxious" who is merely mildly anxious, for the implicit comparison is to our expectations or to average persons. It would be better to describe him as "mildly anxious" or as "anxious, but no more than most."

Ordinary language description distinguishes between cases and contrasts in this important way with those general explanations which are expected to apply across cases; the latter may actually interfere with comparative assessment. Some formulations become standard stock explanations applied by those who rely on them in any and all mental health problems: for some, anxiety or insecurity is the cause of mental health problems; for others, it is an inferiority complex or a poor self-concept. One who relies on such general explanations might observe an aggressive youngster who boldly rules the roost at home and pronounce him insecure, anxious, or suffering from inferiority feelings. But consider the norms: he is not manifestly as insecure as another troubled youngster who stays to himself because he is afraid of people or as insecure perhaps as his "well-adjusted" sister who complies with everyone's expectations for fear of offending. Stating that he is "insecure" might pass as an explanation, but it is misleading for it has no point of reference and does not distinguish this child from other children. It becomes clear that it is no explanation at all when we specify that he is less insecure than others who do not have his problem. It would be better to describe him as bold, aggressive, or insufficiently socialized and to reserve "insecure" for those who are manifestly insecure when compared to other persons.

Stock general explanations which clump problem cases together may be misleading. If the youngster were comparatively insecure, we might suggest support and reassurance, but if he were overly aggressive, then continued reassurance would come to naught and we should rely instead on better ways to control him. Aggressiveness must be described as aggressiveness and not reinterpreted as insecurity, for otherwise the assessment can serve to mislead us.

The objective is to describe the particular characteristics, not to reinterpret them by substituting explanations broad enough to apply to everybody. A wide range of ordinary language concepts is available, and we try to sort through them and choose the right concept from among the many. Assessment requires a sensitivity and alertness, for we must wrestle with the phenomenon and not simply squeeze it into the same tired categories.

Descriptions may apply to a person in some ways in some situations but not in other ways. A man properly described as jealous might be jealous of the fellows who show interest in his attractive teenage daughter, but not jealous at all of other men who talk to his wife. A woman who lacks confidence with anyone who is a potential sweetheart might have considerable confidence with friends or business associates. It is important to specify the range of situations in which the descriptions apply or do not apply. Our initial impressions may be quite skimpy, and we should elaborate on them as more information becomes available.

Clarify multiple meanings: Many words may have more than one meaning, and we must consider what the client means by what he says. A young man confused by his fiancee's actions might say that she is really sensitive, leaving it to us to interpret this. The term "sensitive" has two distinct meanings: it translates as empathic (understanding others and being concerned for them) and also as touchy (thin skinned, easily upset, and too involved with one's own insecurities to be really concerned with others). Perhaps the young man could see that she is really touchy but calls her "sensitive" instead as a euphemism to avoid seeming too harsh on her. It is easier for him to remain ambiguous, and we must clarify the situation for ourselves and for the client as well.

Someone who says he did not "intend" to do something may mean that it was quite inadvertent and accidental, or he may mean that he was not conscious of wanting to do it, that he had not planned to do it, that he wishes now he had not done it, or simply that he should not be held responsible. We must interpret the statement in the light of the client's own semantics. Also, we should avoid saying to a client that he did something intentionally if he would interpret this to mean that he was wrong and we are holding him fully responsible. We might better say that he had legitimate reasons for doing it and was acting on those reasons.

We may need to translate somewhat when clients are using concepts which are confused, faulty, or merely at variance from standard usage. Ordinary language or our explicit common language system provides the template against which the clients' concepts can be readily compared and clarified. The use of ordinary language concepts facilitates communication, for the concepts we use and those of our clients are indeed quite similar. Clients are familiar already with our assessment categories, and we with theirs. By conducting psychotherapy in ordinary language, we facilitate those clarifications which are needed and maintain a mutually understandable basis of communication.

Collaborate

Assessment, like other aspects of psychotherapy, involves close collaboration between therapist and client. The client has been unable to understand herself adequately on her own; yet we must rely closely on her involvement and judgment in our attempts to understand her.

Ask for the Particulars. Even clients with their own quite unrealistic interpretations of things can often relate the actual statements in a conversation accurately enough for us to get a more realistic flavor of what is going on. The clients are seeing the statements but misinterpreting the significance of the actions. The client gives his interpretation of the events, and we ask, "What did you actually say to him?" or "What did he actually say which made it seem that way?" Often it becomes clear that the client is drawing conclusions which follow only tenuously, if at all, from the actual interaction. We use the particulars along with the situational context to better estimate the significance of the actions in question; then we take our conclusions back to the client.

In this way, therapist and client each contribute something essential which the other would otherwise be unable to attain. The client, since he was there, can contribute the particulars that would otherwise be inaccessible, and since we are more experienced and are in a position to be more objective, we can better interpret the meaning of the acts.

Suggest Plausible Interpretations Most clients can conceive of only a limited range of possibilities on their own. Their conclusions reflect the limited possibilities they consider: they arrive at these conclusions not because these square with their observations better than the alternatives, but because they do not even consider the alternatives. We can see other possibilities, but we must enlist the clients' aid to weigh and evaluate them. We suggest alternative interpretations, and invite our clients to give their impressions and to bring forth whatever information they have for or against these interpretations. Clients who would not think of these possibilities on their own can nonetheless contribute a great deal to help sort through and evaluate them when we suggest them. We, as therapists, contribute the alternatives which the clients have overlooked; the clients contribute further information which is essential to weigh those alternatives adequately.

A woman client is hurt by a friend's turning against her and concludes automatically that it happened because she herself had been rude or had done something wrong. She assumes that others' intentions are always good and has not considered that the friend might be jealous of her new lover. We introduce jealousy as a possibility and ask then if it fits. Is this companion a foul weather friend who stands solidly behind you when things go wrong but turns nasty when you start to win? Does she have obvious reason to be jealous? Is she jealous of others? The client contributes the additional information, and together we try to figure out whether jealousy is the answer. There might be other interpretations of the incident as well, and we suggest any which seem to fit. We need not be sure of an interpretation before we introduce it. We introduce interpretations which are plausible and then rely on a collaborative process to evaluate their adequacy. Our participation is essential, for answers given by clients without our assistance may be narrow and quite inadequate to the tasks at hand.

Agreement is not taken as a final indication that an interpretation is adequate, nor disagreement as a final counter indication.. Those clients who try to be cooperative might agree sometimes without having really weighed the ideas, and clients usually disagree when interpretations appear threatening, prejudicial, or otherwise unacceptable. We must weigh these factors in evaluating their responses. We may minimize spurious objections by legitimizing characteristics and by crafting our interpretations to make them as acceptable as possible to the clients. Understanding, objection, or a puzzled expression to an interpretation properly legitimized can be a good indication of its accuracy.

By introducing the possibilities, we structure what the clients will consider, and we must recognize that it is possible thereby to prejudice their answers. But we need not ensure that the clients' answers remain completely unaffected by our interpretations, for we have an ongoing relationship in which artifacts so introduced can be identified as such and steps can be taken to correct them. The purity of our assessments is not as important as their adequacy. We must collaborate to reach adequate formulations of the problems and manage as best we can any wrinkles introduced by our assessment methods.

Monitor Judgment To assess judgment we look at the ways the client sizes up things and the reasons he has for his actions.

We see how his understanding fits the available information and note apparent errors. We see his reasons and compare them to reasons which would be appropriate to someone in such circumstances. The client might weigh factors too heavily which should not be that important or miss factors which truly need to be considered. Poor judgment is shown when someone acts on considerations which are inconsequential or inappropriate to the existing circumstances and ignores more essential considerations.

We monitor judgment as the client tells of what he has done, and we explore with him the reasons he has which weigh into those actions. Some actions which initially seem questionable might be seen as more appropriate in the light of the ways he is viewing things, and others might be seen as more problematic. Our own personal judgment is involved, of course, for we must make estimates of which considerations seem important enough and should weigh into appropriate action. While no one is conscious of all his reasons, most clients are able to contribute many of the considerations that go into their actions. We make better sense of our clients as we listen to the ways they make sense of themselves.

Some schools expect the client to generate the answers on his own and avoid introducing any information into the process for fear of prejudicing the client's answers, like the opinion pollster who avoids saying anything which might suggest an answer to the respondent. Others, in contrast, make their assessments independently and avoid sharing their impressions with the client, anticipating that the client would have little to contribute and might misunderstand the information or be offended by it. The collaborative methods suggested here stand midway between these two extremes.

Recreate Episodes We may gain more information by having the client involve himself more fully with the situations, experiences, and actions of interest. We promote this by having the client play out particular experiences and by watching him interact in a session with family or friends.

We might invite the client to actually enact a scene which he has been concerned about. Perhaps he would speak to a parent as if that person were actually there and then play the response he would expect from that person. Perhaps he could enact the scene including what he might say and also what he would want to say but could not say under the actual circumstances. Enactment involves someone more fully and may bring forth more information than merely talking about the concerns.

Recreating episodes is the mainline procedure in psychodrama, and is used extensively in Gestalt and related dramatic techniques such as family sculpting. Some orientations which rely heavily on recreating things may see this as therapeutically complete in itself and not consider anything more directive to manage the wealth of issues which are brought forth. The suggestion here is to recreate episodes for assessment purposes, and then feel free to use a range of other procedures to manage what is uncovered.

We can also recreate key episodes by inviting intimates into the sessions and having them address key issues. A husband who complains that he and his wife do not fight properly might not be aware how things go wrong when they try to argue. He knows things are going wrong, but there are critical actions that he is overlooking and thus does not understand and cannot tell us. He can give his limited observations and we can estimate other factors from those, but such an assessment might remain too sketchy. To really see what is going wrong, we should invite the wife into the sessions: we might ask what they have disagreed about recently and invite each of them to state his or her positions on the matter. We find out immediately what happens when they attempt to fight. Perhaps each accuses the other and complains about how miserable he is, but neither is willing to risk saying what he wants from the other. We can clarify what is happening and ask each to say what he wants, instead of what he feels he must endure. From there, we can see quite quickly how willing each is to go along with the other and find out what objections stand in the way of change.

Having both parties present allows us to recreate what happens when they fight, but cautions are in order against allowing the fight to continue as it would outside the session. Being accused and condemned raises insecurities and anger quite rapidly, so that clients become too interested in protecting themselves and retaliating against their antagonist to focus seriously on finding mutually compatible solutions. Our strategy is to allow the fight to continue only for the few moments it takes to see what happens, to stop the fight before anyone is seriously harmed, and then to take control and redirect attention to finding solutions. Recreating an argument is a way to assess, but it is not generally therapeutic by itself. The parties who are present can be enlisted to contribute to the solutions.

Friends in a session can be extremely helpful-it is surprising how much a best friend can enrich our understanding of what is going on. Sometimes close friends offer highly accurate observations, and sometimes confused or distorted statements which indicate that the friends are themselves part of the problems. In either case we know better what is going on, and friends as well as family can be enlisted to contribute to the solutions.

Behavioral and of course family therapy orientations include the family as a standard method of assessment. Those who do not invite family or friends to at least one session are missing out on a valuable source of information.

Learn as you go

There is a sensitive interplay between assessment and intervention: some initial assessment provides a basis for choosing appropriate interventions; and the way the client responds to those interventions yields further information and suggests critical questions for additional assessment. The interplay between the two is continual throughout any sequence of therapeutic sessions, so that assessment and intervention are not separate phases but co-occurrences relying, supporting, and building upon one another.

Interweave Assessment and Intervention The position of assessment suggested here contrasts with what is familiar from medical practice in which assessment and treatment are usually separate phases, with assessment completed before treatment begins and little further assessment required unless something unexpected is uncovered. Assessment in psychotherapy belongs not as a stage separate from and prior to therapeutic interventions but as an integral aspect of the entire psychotherapy process. The present chapter on assessment is placed as it is here in the middle of the chapters on intervention guidelines to underscore the position of assessment across the psychotherapy process.

Our main objective in the first moments of an initial session is to make the client comfortable and to establish an alliance. We begin this prior to any formal assessment, and keep an eye out for what creates a comfortable atmosphere and casts us as allies. The client soon brings up some of what is going wrong, or we inquire, and the focus turns to exploring the problems. But as we assess we also work to make things more acceptable to the client, to further establish the alliance, and also to legitimize and in other ways accredit the strengths the client reveals. Thus, from the very beginning and as strongly as possible, we blend in therapeutic statements as we begin our assessment procedures.

We should begin to intervene to clarify and resolve issues as soon as we have a good sense of where to go with these sorts of interventions. We require information sufficient for the initial interventions, but not thorough and complete information on every aspect of all the existing problems. As we play out those initial interventions, we are free to turn again to assessment to pick up additional information which might suggest further or alternate interventions. When the initial interventions are successful, we look to further problem areas, and when unsuccessful, to further or alternate interpretations which suggest to us alternate strategies.

Too many practitioners shy away from early interventions for fear of making some frighteningly irretrievable error. Some caution is appropriate, but one can too easily become overly cautious. Small mistakes are usually not serious unless a therapist becomes stubborn and continues with them too long. Interpretations and interventions should be offered as suggestions anyway rather than as the final word from on high, and those which are not accepted by the client can be sidelined or altered with no harm done.

Most clients appreciate early therapeutic interventions, and it increases their confidence in the therapeutic process. Sometimes clients offer minor problems initially to see if we understand and can help with those problems, and then open up with their more major concerns after sufficient confidence has been built. In crisis intervention cases the immediate problem is readily revealed, but some crisis clients do not continue after the initial crisis is resolved, and there are many clients with little commitment who do not continue past a few sessions anyway. It is especially important with these people to intervene early so that something of value might be attained in the first sessions. Those who do not return may benefit nonetheless, and others who are uncertain might be swayed by seeing that therapy does indeed do some good. It would be an obvious mistake with these clients to devote the initial sessions entirely to assessment.

Supervisors and case conferences too frequently expect a complete assessment of the case, thus pressuring the presenting therapists to spend their first sessions gathering sufficient information to answer enough of the possible questions to avoid appearing unprepared. It would set a better atmosphere in case conferences to ask the presenting therapist what he did in the first session that was effective or at least therapeutically promising, so that trainees learn to sort and grasp promptly some key factors in a case and to move quickly into therapeutic interventions.

Assess through Interventions We can learn from the interventions that others have tried. With a woman who complains continually that nobody understands her, we might ask how her husband or her friends respond when she tells them about the problem. Perhaps they ask her why she feels that way, or sympathize and try to reassure her, or perhaps they become frustrated themselves and tell her it's not so and not to talk that way. The responses which others are already giving are not doing a great deal of good, and by finding out the ways others are failing we can avoid falling into the same mistakes ourselves.

It is becoming more common to see clients who have been seen previously by other therapists, and we should learn from those earlier experiences. Some obvious questions include, "What are some of the things that your previous therapist talked to you about?" "What did he (or she) say which you thought was most helpful?" "What did he say which you felt was insensitive or wrong?" Perhaps some of the previous interventions have been helpful, but others have not gone far enough or have miscarried and caused problems. Through questions such as these, we gain some understanding of what the clients benefit or fail to benefit from, what they approve of, what they find objectionable or intolerable in a therapist. Perhaps a couple terminated with the last therapist because he did not seem to listen to what they were saying or perhaps because he listened all the time but did not talk. Maybe they left their last therapist because he felt they were badly mismatched and should separate; from this we learn that they are not ready to accept that sort of suggestion and will not tolerate a therapist who has that in mind. We do well to look at previous therapeutic attempts so that we might avoid repeating the same mistakes.

Many aspects of problems reveal themselves only as we begin to intervene. Current maladaptive patterns indicate restrictions in the client's ability to do something else which would work out better, but how embedded are those restrictions? Is it just that he has not thought of something better but would jump at it when he saw it, or is he so firmly stuck in his current patterns that he would be unable even to consider what would appear to us to be fairly obvious alternatives? We find out as we suggest that the client try out adaptive alternatives. A husband fails to compliment his wife, but could he do so relatively easily? We ask that he turn to her and compliment her on something she has done. If he cannot think of anything, then we suggest something and ask that he try it. If he is yet unwilling or unable, then that indicates a more stubborn problem. Perhaps he feels awkward complimenting her, or unmanly and weak; perhaps he is angry and sulking at her for neglecting him sexually, and so is strongly disinclined to appreciate her or pay a compliment. Perhaps he agrees and does give her a compliment, but she remains reserved and complains that he is just saying that because he is supposed to, but he does not really mean it. In this case, our attention turns next to what would it take for the wife to accept his compliments.

We sometimes phrase our suggestions to make them assessment questions as well. We might vary the standard "You might want to tell her more of how you are feeling" to make it a question: "What would it take for you to tell her more of how you are feeling?" The latter phrasing is both a suggestion to do something and acknowledgment that the client may be unable as yet to follow the suggestion, and an invitation to talk about the difficulties.

The nature and severity of the impediments to change can sometimes be "guesstimated" ahead of time, but they show themselves most easily, and are most readily explored, as we suggest changes and then continue by finding out what is holding things up. Therapeutic interventions are one of the major ways in which we learn what is holding things up and thus are primary methods of assessment. In many cases there is simply no way to find out ahead of time, and we must rely heavily on what we learn as we intervene.

Everything need not be included in our initial assessment—only enough to suggest an initial therapeutic direction. We should begin with the simplest plausible assessment of the problems and gear our interventions to address those problems. We introduce elaborations and further complexities into the assessment as additional leverage is needed. Initial impressions are sometimes altered, but almost always elaborated upon and expanded continually, over the course of psychotherapy.

The key factors that we should attempt to change are those which have a major impact on the overall pattern and which are most readily altered through something we are in a position to do. But often we must begin interventions aimed at several different factors before we come upon one or more which yield readily and which make an overall difference. We learn which factors are the key ones through our interventions as we try in a number of areas and see what works. Failures provide further information, and therapeutic successes provide some pragmatic validation of our assessments and complementary intervention strategies. We must learn as we go, for much of the critical information is simply not available prior to initial interventions.

Early interventions are characteristic in crisis intervention and in several of the more active therapies. Brief assessment, early intervention, and assessment through intervention require quick judgment and considerable confidence, and may be more characteristic of experienced than of inexperienced therapists.[52]

Don't expect the client to be somebody else.

The problems clients have are oftentimes subtle and complex, and not adequately grasped by our initial assessments or overcome by our initial interventions. It is only natural to want the client to respond to our programs in a constructive manner, and it is too tempting to hold him responsible when he fails to do so. The reminder here is that we must adapt our programs to fit the capacities and inclinations of individual clients, rather than expect them to be the sorts of persons who are to benefit from our most standard intervention tactics. It is up to us to work with the sort of persons the clients actually are, rather than to expect them to be the sort with whom it would be easy for us to work.

Any expectation that clients should understand, readily agree to, and cooperate with whatever we suggest is simply unrealistic. Clients may indeed be quite impossible when one tries to manage them in the standard ways and they will frustrate therapists who cannot adapt. Persons do not sign on as clients in order to fulfill our expectations. Clients become clients in the first place because they are not adapting well to the ordinary conventional ways in which things are done. Their confusions and uncooperative attitudes are not merely impediments to solving the problems-in real ways they are the problems. In treating maladjusted people, the limitations caused by the maladjustments surely must be considered.

We may contribute perfectly good interpretations and suggestions, and find that a client fails to accept our interpretations or follow our suggestions. It is too easy here to become vaguely annoyed and to expect the client to get with it by showing that we really mean business, but if he were the sort of person who could profit from those interpretations and suggestions, then he would not be who he is but someone else better suited to profit from those interpretations and suggestions. We must see therapeutic failures not as indications of bad faith but as opportunities to reevaluate our assessment and to further understand the client's problems.

Many programs appear excellent, but the clients do not respond as expected. It is too easy to continue to expect clients to respond anyway and then consider it their own responsibility when they do not. When apparently excellent programs fail, we must reassess and adapt or alter the programs to suit the clients. A standard quid pro quo marriage approach suggests that husband and wife should each agree to give something, in exchange for getting something they really want. It is a good program, but many clients do not comply. Many of those who feel wronged and mistreated are motivated so strongly to get even that it is anathema to even consider a cooperative program which benefits their antagonists. The major motivations are toward retaliation and against cooperation. Rather than continue to expect such a person to cooperate anyway, we would do well to acknowledge the failure and to explore its basis. We might legitimize the problem by saying: "After the way he has treated you, why should you want to do something that would benefit him? That must feel like letting him get away with it." The retaliatory interests can be explored, and perhaps resolved or rechanneled, but it is foolish to expect cooperation from husbands and wives whose main interests are in getting even.

Preconceptions can contribute to unrealistic expectations. A humanist who sees persons as wholly good may fail to acknowledge that persons do purposeful harm to others. Everyday experience teaches us that persons are complex enough to intend both good and harm to others, and a preconception of simple goodness restricts one's ability to see the darker side of human action. One who expects clients to be always motivated to cooperate and make things work out is expecting them to be other than how they really are. Ideally everyone should be

willing to cooperate to make things work out best for everybody, but not everyone conforms to these ideals.

One who expects others to be some other way may be attempting to require them to live up to his expectations. It is a way of exerting social pressure. But clients do not straighten out merely because we expect them to do so, for they have limited capacities which must be overcome. One who expects clients to overcome limitations they cannot overcome may be doing so in order to avoid responsibility himself for figuring out what would make things work. Requiring clients to do things they cannot do is a sure path to therapeutic failure.

Questions are too often asked which are well beyond what the client can reasonably answer, and we should avoid asking unanswerable questions. One way to estimate whether the question is answerable is to ask yourself what would qualify as an answer and then ask yourself if the client can come up with something like that himself. We should be able to see at least one plausible answer to any question. Should the client find the question too vague, we can suggest plausible answers, and invite him to weigh and choose between them. If you cannot come up with anything that would qualify as an answer, then that indicates that the client probably cannot either. Suggesting plausible answers is the major way to avoid asking unanswerable questions.

The following exchange between a frustrated psychotherapist and an inveterate alcoholic provides a parody of an unanswerable question:

Therapist: So what are you going to do to stop drinking?
Alcoholic: Gee, sir, I don't know.

Therapist: Well, think about it, and tell me in the morning what you figure out.

Therapist and alcoholic have not "figured it out" in the entire session together, and it should be quite clear that the alcoholic is not going to produce the answer magically on his own. The therapist expects the client to do something he has already shown himself incapable of doing, perhaps to avoid facing squarely the obvious impasse. It would be better to acknowledge that they have failed to find a reasonable facsimile of a solution.

It is our responsibility to adapt our programs to our clients rather than expecting them to be properly adaptable to our programs. This is not to advocate that we try to work with any and all clients, or even that we struggle forever with those clients we do take on. Not all clients can respond to the things we know how to do, for there are limits to our personal competencies as therapists and limits to the art of psychotherapy regardless of who is conducting it. Some clients show themselves to be unresponsive to everything we know how to do, and we should not continue and expect them to respond anyway when they have shown they cannot. Acknowledging the limitations to our competencies is not the same thing as holding the clients responsible for the failures. In addition, cost effectiveness and personal preferences must be considered: we might choose to work less with those who respond slowly if at all and to focus instead on those who respond more rapidly to therapy. We might focus on those with whom we are more personally compatible. As therapists, we should take responsibility for improving our competencies, but nobody should expect to treat every client successfully. We must accept responsibility for our choices of where and to whom we commit our energies.

8
Clarifications

Clarify existing situations and clarify the means by which one might attempt to change these situations:

Clarify situations.
Clarify key concepts.
Deal with the reality basis of emotions.
.

CLARIFY SITUATIONS

What you understand or misunderstand about your situation contributes directly to your experiences and actions. What you take to be real provides the boundaries for what you might be concerned with and want to do something about. Inadequate or mistaken observation is a basis for inappropriate responses and is a contributing factor in most psychological problems. Clarification of the situations in which one lives is essential in the therapeutic process.

Separate Your Own Contributions. In many cases the client is contributing so much to foul up relationships that it is impossible for him to assess properly how others would behave under more ordinary conditions. A wife who complains that her husband does not speak to her and then ices him every chance she gets leaves us with an open question about him: Is he incapable of a more involved relationship, or is he simply responding to her aloofness and resentment? Sometimes an answer can be estimated from available information. Is the husband more involved with others than he is with her, or is he generally uncommunicative with everyone? Has he ever been more involved with her; if so, under what circumstances? Has he responded when she has been warm to him, or has he remained silent?

We might also have the client clear up his or her contributions to the relationship problems and from there seeing if the partner is capable of changing. In this case, the woman might be coached to be warmer and see if it does make a difference. Changes can be suggested for each partner should both of them be involved in the sessions, so that the process seems fairer and more palatable. In this manner, we clarify important relationships by having the clients change and then seeing how others respond. If the wife here is unwilling to make such changes, she limits how much she will know about her husband: she cannot know how he would be to a warmer wife. And proper caution suggests that we too wait for real evidence before drawing conclusions about what sort of person he would be in a warmer marriage.

The same issue is seen in various forms. A client who is himself unassertive is often taken advantage of by family and friends. If the client were to stand up for himself, would those others become more considerate, or would they simply ignore the assertive requests and fight harder to stay in control? One good way to find out is to encourage assertiveness and see how others react. With those who accept your rights when you state them forcefully, there are opportunities for improved relationships, but not with those who are unyielding. An assessment principle introduced earlier is to intervene actively and see how our clients respond. The same principle is applied here to help the client see clearly those persons who are important in his life: encourage the client to act in improved ways so that he can see how others respond.

Weigh Alternatives with the Client

Often single observations can be interpreted more than one way, so that one needs to consider alternate interpretations and weigh several observations to piece together what is going on. Involved here is a process of

143

reasoning from available observations to arrive at conclusions best fitted to the overall configuration of information. Our objective as therapists is not merely to arrive at the answers, but to improve the abilities of the clients to reason through similar problems in similar ways. The process requires considerable sensitivity and judgment, which are best transmitted by having the client participate actively in the entire reasoning process. It is a mistake to figure things out ourselves and then lay on the client our startling and ingenious conclusions. We should go through the reasoning process step by step in collaboration with the client and thus arrive jointly at some reasonable conclusions. In so doing, we familiarize our clients with the steps it takes to arrive at good conclusions and thereby improve their abilities to do so themselves.

When family or friends are included in the sessions, the process is made easier for we can see directly what those persons are saying and doing, and can share our impressions. By so doing, our clients see what we consider as important and how we interpret things.

Legitimize Misunderstandings. We clarify the specific paths by which the client is arriving at his wrong conclusions and so make sense of his misperceptions. In so doing, we accredit the client as rational despite his errors and gain further advantage: as the structure of sensibleness becomes clear, the particular errors stand out in contrast, and can more easily be analyzed and reevaluated.

The client may have a vested interest in particular views or may be threatened by more realistic alternatives. In some cases our conclusions are literally unthinkable to the client, for were things that way then familiar pillars of security would be shaken and foundations would have to be constructed anew. We can lend some credibility to our conclusions here by mentioning the limitation: "To you, it is unthinkable that this could be so." By this simple move, we avoid confrontation on whether or not it is so, and direct the conversation instead to

144

that which limits the client's ability to consider it even as a possibility. In so doing we legitimize the client's failure to consider an alternative viewpoint.

Emphasize Understanding over Misunderstandings Alternative approaches are available to try to redress misunderstandings: one might comment first to clarify the situation itself, so that the person can get a more realistic view of the situation and from there see that he had been misunderstanding it; or one can comment first that the person is misunderstanding things, so that he can look at his misunderstandings and change them. Several considerations suggest that we begin by clarifying that which is to be understood.

Identifying something as a misunderstanding is generally a two-step process: one who understands something a particular way attains an apparently more reliable observation, and then identifies the first view as less reliable and mistaken in comparison to the second. The most apparent quality of a misunderstanding is that is falls short by comparison to some other view which is taken to be more reliable.

Consider the issue in seeing others as trustworthy or untrustworthy. With a husband who is suspicious of his wife and sees her as untrustworthy, we begin in our assessment with an obvious question: Is she untrustworthy? Only as we answer that can we understand whether he is misperceiving his wife's actions or perceiving them accurately. Suppose she is faithful to him and concerned with his best interests, so that his failure to see her as trustworthy shows him to be an overly suspicious individual. It is on the basis of viewing her as less conniving than he sees her to be that we conclude he is misperceiving the matter.

In what ways might we best enable him to overcome this problem? An initial tactic is to take the client through the same reasoning processes that anyone must go through to identify a misperception. We might analyze with him the wife's actions, weigh plausible interpretations, and draw the conclusion that her actions in themselves do or do not suggest unfaithfulness. Whether agreeing or disagreeing with our conclusion, he can see that we have taken the issue seriously, and he generally appreciates the consideration and thoroughness of the analysis. Often the person can understand the reasoning but is unable to actually see things that way; in such cases, he can see his own perceptions as misperceptions, and is more apt to cooperate with the sometimes lengthy task of changing those perceptions.

The overall objective must be to clarify the situation itself, rather than to clarify misunderstandings of the situation. Should the husband come to see his wife as trustworthy, then whether or not he understands his suspiciousness he has resolved his problems. Should he come to see that he is excessively suspicious but still perceive his wife as unfaithful, then his problem remains in full force and his insight that he is suspicious is of little consequence. Improvement occurs as he comes to see the situation more accurately and not simply as he understands his misunderstanding. It is the ability to see clearly one's situations and relationships which must stand as the critical objective; interpretations of misinterpretations are only one of the ways of accomplishing that objective.

The client here is too untrusting, but the issue is broader and more complex than that. Aside from whether he should trust more or take more risks, the issue is primarily one of judgment. Whom should he trust, in what circumstances, and to what extent? What sort of risks are involved, and how does he recover without too much grief if someone fails him? Focus on the relationship factors for or against trusting invites the client to look beyond his introspective inadequacies and to begin to see the real world complexities so essential for good judgment. The issue is whom and when to trust, and that must be answered whether or not someone identifies himself as too untrusting. It is important to look at specific relationships and understand them on an individual basis. Some persons may be found to warrant more trust than one is giving; others, less trust. The major issue is in making the distinctions, and extremely suspicious persons have as much or more difficulty as anyone else in telling the difference between trustworthy and untrustworthy companions.

One might analyze situations and thereby clarify misinterpretations, and one might analyze misinterpretations and thereby clarify the situations which are being misinterpreted. Each has its place so long as they are the means to the primary objective, which is to enable the client to see clearly the situational realities that he is facing.

The principle here to first clarify situations is suggested by several orientations but contrasts to that of other familiar schools. Behavioral orientations emphasize objective measurement, reality therapy clarifies the reality of existing situations, and family orientations look firsthand at what actually happens in the intimate relationships. A good many eclectics tend to focus first on situational realities and from there try to redress confusions and misunderstandings about those realities. In contrast, analytic and dynamic traditions interpret misperceptions but underemphasize situational realities; Gestalt unfolds the complexities of the client's views but does not suggest more realistic views; client-centered accepts without questions whatever interpretations the client makes; and phenomenologists emphasize individual experiences over the actual situations. These latter schools focus primarily on what the client sees and experiences, and secondarily or not at all on what is there to be seen.

Clarify key concepts

Concepts are those distinctions we use to order our world. The clarification of everyday concepts provides a sturdy foundation for our common language approach to psychotherapy, and we naturally advocate the same good foundations for our clients. Clients who are using concepts which are inadequate or confounded by extraneous meanings are restricted in their abilities to figure things out. Progress is often gained through clarification and improvement of key concepts.

Elaborate Impoverished concepts Troubled persons tend to use concepts which distinguish things in queer ways and thus misshape reality. The concept of "selfishness" provides a good example, since it is an important issue in social relationships and is often misunderstood. Selfishness for many troubled persons means standing up for oneself, taking care of oneself, or merely finding enjoyment in something. Thus, finding satisfaction in life means being selfish. Such persons, to avoid being selfish, avoid pleasures or feel ashamed when they do enjoy themselves.

Too frequently, practitioners attempt to challenge such problems by telling the client that it is good to be selfish and that he should feel free to be selfish. This sort of solution accepts the existing misconstrued concept and turns it backwards: accepting that enjoyment is selfish, and that that selfishness is right and good rather than wrong. The solution violates our commonsense understanding that selfishness is wrong and so invites confusion, failure, and possibly narcissism or, in plain language, selfishness.

A better solution clarifies the key concept. We might begin with a simple statement of what selfishness means, such as, "Selfishness means taking more than your share at somebody else's expense," and from there apply the concept appropriately to the client's situation: "When you do things you enjoy you feel it is selfish, but in order to qualify you must take more than your share so that somebody else misses out. There is no such thing as more than your share of enjoyment, for there is enough for everyone who seeks it. When you enjoy yourself you are more pleasant to be around, but when you are miserable you make others miserable too, so in that sense there is even some social good in enjoying yourself." Applying the concept to the client's situation is helpful. One young woman, for instance, feels that it would be selfish of her to ask her husband to do things in their lovemaking especially to please her, but she resents his inconsiderateness. He, on the other hand, would love nothing better than to please her. One might comment: "You feel it would be selfish to ask for what you want, but it would please him greatly for you to do just that. When you find pleasure in your lovemaking, you give him pleasure. It would be generous of you, and not selfish, since by asking for what you want you would please him as well as yourself."

Sometimes by looking out for ourselves we might cheat others, but this is not generally so, and in many cases we even enrich the lives of those around us. A failure to see the difference is a clear limitation. By enabling a client to make distinctions such as this, we open up new possibilities for more sensible actions.

Untangle Confounded Concepts

An individual may include extraneous meanings in the distinctions he makes and thus confuse critical issues. Concepts which include extraneous meanings might be termed confused, over-inclusive, or confounded concepts: the extraneous meanings obscure the critical distinctions.

One might have a concept for instance of marriage as entrapment, of success as selling out to the establishment, or of suffering as a sign of love. In confounded concepts the one thing means the other, so that there is no separating them: marriage means entrapment, is always entrapment, and cannot be seen otherwise. Appropriate concepts in contrast allow one to make the available distinctions: some marriages are entrapping, and others are quite freeing. Confounding is involved when an individual sees all marriage as entrapment and is unable to conceive of marriage which is not entrapment or to see it that way when it is in front of his eyes. Marriage means entrapment, and the concept is binding upon his view of reality.

Confounded concepts such as these are frequent sources of problems. A young man, for instance, who has made plans to marry might find himself beset with insecurities, and feeling that the freedom and joy of life are gone. Little does it matter that he and the woman have spent many enjoyable hours together, that she loves him dearly, or even that they have been living together in a relationship which is marriage in all but formal legal sanction. The same woman who has been so pleasant as a sweetheart and companion is now to be a wife-an agent of the oppressive system of entanglements-and he, who so enjoys his freedom, is to become a husband. His concept of marriage is binding on the participants. Anticipation through misconstrued concepts casts a sense of gloom over the coming changes and tends to reconstruct the relationship so that it fulfills his expectations of it.

We begin here in the most obvious manner, by making explicit the misconstrued concepts: "To you, marriage means entrapment. Your concept of marriage is that it is entrapment, and you cannot see it any other way." We attempt to clarify the concept for the client by outlining variations that marriage might take and by asking the client to look into them: "What would a marriage be like in which there was warmth and love?" "What except your own expectations keeps you from continuing as marrieds with the same friendship you shared as lovers?" "Have you ever seen a good marriage? Would you recognize one if you saw it?"

Legitimizing the confusion is usually a step in untangling it. Suppose the young man grew up in a family in which his parents sulked, moped, and appeared miserable but stayed together, as the story goes, for the children. The upbringing might be used to legitimize his perceptions, as follows: "Your main exposure has been to your parents' marriage; you saw the miserableness and entrapment, and that there was no escape. It is not so surprising that you have come to see marriage as entrapment and are wary of it." By legitimizing the misconception, we show the client the sense he makes to have the views he has and also open the way for reconsidering those views. One marriage is not a good enough sample for all marriages, and other possibilities can be considered.

Confounded concepts such as these are common. Steps to clarify them are to make explicit the extraneous meanings, to suggest a clearer concept and draw attention to supportive considerations, and to legitimize the original misconstrued concept. The clarification of confounded concepts opens possibilities for the client to better structure reality. The clarification of inadequate concepts resolves problems in some cases, although in other cases the problems are more embedded and do not yield. Either way the clarification is a good beginning in that it provides an initial understanding of the problems and suggests some further paths to explore.

The clarification of the client's concepts is included in some cognitive approaches and is the major focus in personal construct psychotherapy.[53] But there is too little concern generally with the analysis and clarification of those everyday concepts used by the clients, perhaps because so many orientations push their own theory-based concepts as replacements for everyday concepts.

Deal with the reality basis of emotions

The client's situation as he sees it is a major contributing factor to the feelings and emotions he experiences. There are really two factors involved here: the situation as it actually is, and the client's perceptions and misperceptions of his situation. One reacts to the way things are, but one reacts more specifically and immediately to the way one perceives things to be. Perceptions themselves are understandable from the actual situation and from the individual's distinctive ways of seeing and interpreting things.

An individual's situation as he sees it is a major contributing factor to his feelings and emotions, and also to the actions he takes to deal with his situation. So one major way to influence someone is to influence what he perceives, and to accomplish this, there are two major therapeutic paths. (1) To the extent that the client misperceives his situation and sees it as worse than (or merely different than) it really is, our task then is to clarify with him the existing situation and enable him to perceive it more accurately. (2) To the extent that the client is in an uncomfortable situation and is accurately perceiving how things are, our task is to clarify ways in which he might more effectively manage the situation and perhaps change it to suit him better. The objective either way is to deal with the reality basis of the emotions: in the former case, we clarify what the reality basis actually is; in the latter, we clarify ways to change it.

With a client who is lonely we might convey that we accept and understand the feelings of loneliness, but there is only so much that can be accomplished with this response. The major focus should be on the reality basis of those feelings, so that the essential question is, "In what sense are you really alone, and what can you do about it?" One who is lonely generally sees himself as having no close friends or as being separated from those who are important. Perhaps there are others near who have friendly feelings about him, but the person is wary or considers others beneath him and himself above them, so that he fails to appreciate available friendships: he needs to see more clearly that there are friendships available and that it is his attitude toward others which causes his loneliness. Perhaps, on the other hand, the person is socially introverted, knows few people, and is afraid to meet anyone: in such cases the person needs encouragement and perhaps training to become more active socially, in order to meet others and make friendships. The therapeutic task either way is to deal not merely with the feelings but also with the perceptions and situational realities which are the basis of those feelings.

There is a logical connection between perceptions of situations and feelings and emotions. Perceptions of being friendless or socially isolated go with feelings of loneliness. Anxiety and fear are associated with being threatened or in danger. Anger goes with being provoked or mistreated. Feelings of guilt go with the perception of having done something wrong. These go together because of the logical connections between seeing things in particular ways, and the feelings and emotions one generally has toward those sorts of things 54 .

Situations, perceptions, and emotions in issues of anger and guilt are explored in the following illustration. A young woman is being confused by a highly manipulative relationship with her mother. The young woman fears that she has failed her mother and, more specifically, that she is ungrateful, neglectful, and inconsiderate toward the woman who has given her whole life to raise her. She feels insecure, worthless, and guilty over all the trouble she is causing. She lives with her mother, is conscientious and attentive, and does everything she can to avoid hurting her mother and to make up for everything. She does not understand why she is so fearful and depressed so much of the time. Yet she acquired the attitudes she has through direct inculcation. Her mother complains continually about how much she gives to her daughter and how little she receives in return, most probably in order to obligate and maintain control over her daughter. The mother figures that her daughter owes this to her and fears perhaps that her daughter might abandon her if she allowed her to go her own selfish way.

In brief, the young woman is passive, insecure, and being run over by an angrily manipulative and long-suffering mother. Passivity and compliance in the face of such obvious mistreatment are clearly contributing to the problem, and one major therapeutic objective is to enable this woman to confront her mother, challenge the mistreatment, and take some steps toward normal independence. At the outset, however, suggestions to challenge her mother would be unsuccessful, because she sees the conflicts with her mother as caused by a failure on her own part, and not as caused by manipulation and mistreatment by her mother. The initial step must be to clarify with her the reality basis of the feelings she is having. She needs to understand clearly that she is not inconsiderate but is herself being mistreated, and to see this, she must come to perceive her mother's accusations accurately as inauthentic and manipulative

The initial step, therefore, is to enable her to see through the suffering and accusations, and to understand them for what they are—manipulative attempts to obligate and subordinate her. As long as she perceives the accusations as legitimate, then the acid of those accusations binds her, and she sees herself as guilty and has strong reason to capitulate. When she sees the accusations as manipulative rather than legitimate, then her reasons to capitulate are no longer so strong, and she gains reason to resist. Capitulation makes sense when you are in the wrong, but making a stand makes sense when someone else mistreats and wrongs you. In seeing more clearly the reality of the situation, the young woman gains reason to act more appropriately toward the problems. Clarifying with her the realities of her relationship with her mother may require considerable time and energy, for she would have some investment in the current way of seeing things. Nevertheless, this is an essential objective: she must perceive what is really going on if she is to see the sense in an appropriate way to deal with it.

Assertive stands are generally therapeutic to the extent that they affirm your rights and prevent others from ignoring or mistreating you. But they are not particularly therapeutic when others ignore them and continue to run over you anyway, for that further confirms your impotence. Assertive stands are therapeutic to the extent that they deal effectively with the reality basis of the problems.

Since the woman does not acknowledge or express anger, one might consider that she needs to be able to do so. But at the outset, our interpretations of underlying anger or suggestions that she express anger would gain little. Were we to look only at the mistreatment she is receiving, we would see that she has every right to be angry, and we might assume therefore that she really is angry. But it is important to look not merely at the situation but at her perceptions of the situation, and to match her emotional states to her perceptions. As she sees it, her mother is justified and she herself is the one in the wrong. She says she feels guilty rather than angry, and in recognizing her perceptions, we see that it makes sense for her to feel the way she says she does. She feels guilty because she sees herself as in the wrong, whereas she would feel angry if she were to see herself instead as provoked and mistreated. Perhaps she alternates between feeling guilty and feeling angry, as persons sometimes do, seeing herself alternately as the wrongdoer, then as having been mistreated, and then again as the wrongdoer. Should she get angry, she might take that as further indication that she is ungrateful and in the wrong; so she would quickly suppress the anger, feel guilty about it, and try to make amends for it. When she can see better the reality of the relationship, she will be in a better position to feel emotions that are more appropriate to that reality: when she sees that she is being manipulated and abused, she will feel angry rather than merely guilty and will be able to accept the anger. The anger can then be channeled into assertive counterresponses to the manipulation and intimidation she is facing, for justified anger over the mistreatment would provide additional motivations for assertive stands with her mother.

Note here that the problem is not simply a matter of being unable to express her feelings. It is a matter rather of seeing more clearly the realities of the situation, so that she will have more realistic and appropriate feelings which can serve as motivations for more appropriate actions. The perceptions a person has of his situation contribute directly to his emotional states, and as he comes to see better the realities of his situation, his emotions should become more appropriate to that situation. As he sees things more clearly, he is in a better position to respond to them more appropriately, and feelings and emotions are but one aspect of a more appropriate response. Seeing existing situational realities and dealing appropriately with them go hand in hand, for accurate perceptions and the corresponding appropriate emotions are proper bases for effective action.

Expressing feelings may affect for better or worse the reality basis of those feelings. One who expresses anger over being mistreated may find that others listen, that problems are clarified, and that relationships improve. In other circumstances, one who expresses anger may find that others see him as unjustifiably antagonistic and counter with further antagonism of their own, so that relationships deteriorate and one has more problems than before. Like assertive responses, expressions of anger are therapeutic to the extent that they contribute constructively to the reality basis of the emotions, and not otherwise. Orientations in the analytic and humanistic veins uphold expressing feelings as essential to adequate mental health, whereas others in the behavioral, rational-emotive, and reality therapy traditions see it as vastly overrated and often problematic. Our analysis here suggests a way of integrating the countermanding voices: the expression of feelings is therapeutic when it clarifies and improves the reality basis of those feelings, but not when it confuses or exacerbates things. It is not a matter of freeing oneself from the emotions by expelling them through their expression, but of freeing oneself by dealing constructively with the factors which contribute to and cause the emotions.

Thus, in advocating the expression of emotions, we should be clear about what issues might be clarified and what situations improved in the process. Blind expressions of emotions such as anger, without regard to their effects, may generate too much heat and too little light: it is better to realize what we are getting into. The pragmatic considerations suggest that we encourage expression of feelings when it helps the client accept his feelings, clarifies situations, and improves relationships, but not when it commits him to confused or indulgent positions, antagonizes others, or jeopardizes relationships. "Deal with the reality basis of emotions" was introduced by Ossorio as a policy for psychotherapy.

To deal with the reality basis of emotions we clarify the situations contributing to those emotions and also clarify the ways to change those situations. The two guidelines following explore further the pragmatics of attempting to change situations: the first focuses on the approaches the client is currently using; the second, on generating more effective alternatives that might be used instead.

9
Ways and Means

Any intentional action involves a competency aspect. One acts "in order to" or as a "way to" or a "means to" get something he want, and may or may not know which sort of approach will be successful and what will fail. We look here at the various approaches, particularly the impractical ones which produce such poor outcomes, and how can we influence clients toward more practical approaches.

Clarify misunderstandings how

The know-how or competency aspect of any action might be stated as a premise: That is, for any purposive action, the premise is that that act is a way of attaining the intended objective, and the individual takes it that such acts are the way or at least a way of attaining those things he is after.

For instance, punishing a child in order to make him work harder implies some belief that punishment is a way to make someone work harder. Punishing a child to show that you are superior to him includes some sense that punishment is a way of showing you are superior. Showing upset feelings in order to gain special consideration suggests that you think that showing these feelings is a way to gain special consideration. As for sulking to show how much someone hurt you, you believe that sulking is a safer way to blame someone for hurting you. More generally, for any action there is always the premise that the act is a way to accomplish what it is being done to accomplish.

One of the important quirks of these premises is that they are most generally implicit: as with any know-how or competency issue, you are not generally conscious of the nature of your premise or conscious for that matter that you even have a premise. There is this important contrast between knowing <u>that</u> something is so and knowing how to do something: you are generally quite well aware of the former, but the latter is usually quite inarticulate[55]. As long as premises remain implicit, they are hardly subject to change through conscious consideration.

The effectiveness is the concern here. Some actions are appropriate to what they are done to accomplish, whereas other actions are ineffective or dysfunctional, perhaps even losing for the actor his objectives. In the former, the individual knows how to bring about what he wants, and his approaches are valid ones. In the latter, he misunderstands how, and his premises are invalid and cause problems. When a person has insufficient know how and invalid operating premises, he goes about things in the wrong ways and so fails to attain what he is after.

Our task is to recognize the premises on which the client acts, to clarify and make them conscious for the client, and to evaluate their validity with the client. Where the premises are invalid, our task further is to have the client see this himself so that he no longer uses these ineffective means to get what he seeks.

Some sensitivity may be required to correctly identify implicit premises, and considerable effort may be involved to convince the client to let go of premises which are invalid. One mother becomes extremely upset when her daughter misbehaves, and the mother fails to exercise appropriate authority. An initial therapeutic objective is thus to diminish the mother's upsetness and enable her to exercise authority over her daughter. Straightforward justification of the use of authority and instructions on how to do it have little impact with this woman: the mother contends that the daughter should care more for her and be more considerate. The argument here is that the daughter should see how much her misbehavior is upsetting her mother and should show her love by correcting her conduct. Additional leverage is thus needed, and we might focus on the apparent commitment to being excessively upset. The mother argues that if the daughter realized how much she was hurting her mother, she would not continue to act that way. She thus reveals her operating premise: "Showing her how she is upsetting me should cause her to realize her responsibility for my feelings and to improve her conduct." The upsetness, as the mother sees it, should evoke in the daughter some caring and sense of responsibility, and should cause her to regret her mistakes and act properly. Instead and quite understandably, the daughter sees the weakness, loses respect for her mother, is angered by the manipulation, and uses the opportunity to do as she quite well pleases.

The operating premise is explained to the mother with the daughter present. The mother agrees that she expects her being upset to control her daughter's misbehavior, and she sees that it has not had the expected effect. But she continues to argue that her feelings should mean something to her daughter and seems genuinely baffled that the daughter misbehaves anyway. Our task at this point is to show the mother that her operating premise is invalid, and we might pursue this in one or more of several ways.

We might legitimize the invalid premise. Suppose that when the mother was a youngster, she and her family and friends were compliant and concerned with their parents' feelings, and would go to considerable lengths to avoid hurting their parents' feelings. She learned naturally enough that being upset merits, and indeed gains, special consideration from others and causes others to improve their misconduct. We use her experiences as a youngster to legitimize her premise, for at that time consideration of mother's upset feelings did indeed cause one to correct misconduct. But families change, and youngsters today are more involved with their friends and with television, family authority is weaker, and upset feelings no longer command the compliance they once did. We thus show the mother that she acquired the approach honestly enough, but that it no longer has the same validity in the current modern patterns of family relationships. We might challenge by inviting her to consider the available evidence: "You feel that a youngster who sees how much hurt she is causing, if she loves you, would have to change. Yet you have been upset with her for many years-quite openly and conspicuously upset. Could you conclude that it is not doing the job for you?" We might continue: "If showing how much she upsets you were the golden path to raising responsible children, then Julie would be one of the most conscientious children on the block, for you are certainly one of the most long-suffering of parents."

Finally, we might invite the mother to continue to act on her premise-perhaps even in an accelerated or exaggerated manner-so that through further observations she invalidates for herself her misconceived approach. Such tacks have a paradoxical appearance and are best done with a touch of humor, for example: "Perhaps being upset should cause your youngster to realize her mistakes and change, but maybe you have not yet really given it a fair chance. My opinion is that it will not work, but you are not going to take my word for it. You might want to give it a try for a few more weeks, but this time really do it right. You might show that you are extremely upset by the way she is treating you and lay it on with extra exuberance. Have you tried suggesting that she is going to cause you to have a nervous breakdown? Perhaps something exotic might get her attention."

In addition to controlling misbehavior, several motives may be involved in the commitment to showing upset, such as appearing to be a concerned and loving parent, presenting oneself as so undone already that nobody would dare accuse you of messing up your daughter, or transferring responsibility for failures from yourself to your daughter. Each additional reason for being upset must be addressed on its own.

Clarification of operating premises has important commonalities to some of the philosophies and methods of Eastern enlightenment, in which unexamined premises are seen as major barriers to be reexamined through the requirements of the training. In one "koan," or training problem, the master holds a brick over the apprentice's head and tells the apprentice, "If you speak to me, I will drop this brick on your head. And if you do not speak to me, I will drop this brick on your head." The situation seems impossible: the apprentice reveres the master and wants ever so much to show himself worthy by solving the problem, and in so doing to protect his cranium. Yet either of the alternatives is a sure loss. So what is the apprentice to do? Note that there is an implicit premise here and that the situation is problematic only so long as the premise remains implicit. The premise is that staying seated under the brick is the way to attempt to solve the problem. Once you recognize the premise, then you are in a position to reexamine it. In this case, you easily see that your premise is invalid, and you have solved the koan: you get out from under the brick. The problem is resolved when the premise can be consciously scrutinized.

Many everyday situations appear to offer similar unacceptable alternatives: continue your efforts, or try harder, and fail; or quit and fail. In such cases there is an invalid premise so that efforts are wasted in unconstructive directions, and failure is a constant companion. In some cases, as with the Koan, merely mentioning the invalid premise is sufficient. But in most cases considerable effort is required to clarify and adequately reevaluate the premises. Identifying the operating premise is in all such cases an essential first step in the solution of the problems.

Where the premises are implicit, the client can face failure, and even repeated failure, but remain unable to connect it to the source of the problems. He sees things are going wrong but sees nothing about what is making them go wrong; the result is that he profits not at all from his failures and may be harmed by them. In contrast, when the premises are explicit, the client can connect observed failures to the operating premises and, through such experiences, evaluate and perhaps alter his premises. There is considerable advantage in clarifying the operating premises in our search for solutions to seemingly intractable problems.

In Eastern enlightenment, the method is often to encourage the student to struggle with seemingly intractable problems until he stumbles upon the operating premises which narrow his vision and make solution of the problems impossible. Alan Watts (1961) in Psychotherapy East and West compares the Eastern process to insight-oriented psychotherapies, and focuses on the prevalence of invalid premises:

But what is the guru or therapist to do? ... almost the only thing the guru or therapist can do is to persuade the individual to act upon his false premise in certain consistent directions until he sees his mistake.... For this, as we have seen, was the essential technique of liberation: to encourage the student to explore his false premises consistently-to the end. (pp. 106-107, 78)

The method of Eastern enlightenment is to force the student to struggle on his own until he finds his premises, so that he can reexamine them. Our approach here is tailored to Western ways, in which there is less patience and we are expected to resolve many mis-directions in a finite number of hours. Our approach is an abbreviated version of the Eastern approach: we do not require our clients to struggle for the years it might take to recognize their invalid premises on their own. We clarify and make explicit their operating premises so that they can begin to examine them and go on from there. When clients see the failings of their premises but are still committed to them, we too can recommend that they continue to act on the false premises consistently and with increased effort-to the end.

There are practical advantages in favor of clarifying premises in our search for rapid solutions to particular maladaptive tendencies. We contribute as we can to clarifying operating premises and, from there, consider with the client the appropriateness and validity of those premises. Convincing the client to give up his invalid approaches goes hand in hand with introducing him to more effective alternatives.

Clarify how to

What might the client do instead? Existing approaches are not working, and alternative, more practical ways to approach things are needed. Our task is to find alternative ways to make things work and to clarify for the client how he might approach things in these more effective ways. Clarifying invalid approaches and introducing better alternative approaches go hand in hand, for together these are the practicalities of how things are and are not to be done. Each contributes to helping the client change. Treating the parent who uses being upset to control thus involves two complementary tacks: we convey that being upset is not a viable approach, and we involve the parent in alternatives. In so doing we give her reasons for not continuing to use upsetness and reasons for using something else instead. We might alternate focus between the two in any single session. In order to generate alternatives, we might support the parent and improve her confidence, teach her more effective ways to manage the youngster and to exercise authority, suggest negotiations with the youngster, and so on. It is easiest to give up an invalid approach when one has a more effective alternative to try instead.

Alternatives are best sought cooperatively, by inviting our clients to puzzle through with us what is or is not a more practical way to do things. But we must be willing to introduce the more practical alternatives ourselves, for clients are often unable to do so on their own. Clients who could see for themselves the more effective alternatives would be well on their way already to using them. That clients do not act more expediently already is in itself a good indication that they do not know how to do so.

Suggestions for more practical alternative actions are used in most active psychotherapies. Behavior therapists suggest positive behavior patterns, including assertive actions to affirm one's rights and cooperative actions better suited to gain positive responses; rational-emotive therapists order assertive actions to correct problem situations; planning for more successful action is one of eight major principles of reality therapy; and family orientations suggest complementary changes simultaneously for several members of the family.

Deal with Objections. Clients generally have some reasons against trying available alternatives. The suffering parent who fails to take charge might feel that if she did exercise authority, she would lose control of herself and harm her youngsters, that she would suppress their individuality, or that they would not love her anymore and she would be alone. One who fails to make assertive stands might feel that it is inconsiderate to be so forward, that in doing so he would hurt others' feelings and be responsible for their suffering, or that he would lose their friendship. Such considerations give the person reasons for avoiding the suggested alternatives. These objections are not invented on the spot to foul up our excellent plans for changes. Such reservations have been operative all along, often severely limiting the alternatives the client has been able to consider. Too many stock "yes, but. . . " counters to our suggestions may indicate that we have paid insufficient attention to the client's legitimate objections. To make alternatives viable, it is essential therefore to clarify the client's objections and to answer them sufficiently so that they no longer weigh so strongly against change.

Our task is to address the objections so that we can clarify how many unfavorable outcomes are to be realistically expected and convince the client of the safety of the suggested alternatives. When some unfavorable outcomes might be reasonably anticipated, these need to be weighed against the advantages of the action, and preparations should be made to contain the problems. What if someone does get icy when you take a stand-what do you do then? How long will the chill factor last, and how do you manage it while it is there? We need to take such reservations seriously and construct some answers. Where problems are to be realistically anticipated, an essential question is, Is it worth it? If the alternatives are to make sense, the advantages of the alternatives need to be weighed favorably against the risks.

Often the client is overestimating adverse consequences and needs to view them more realistically. When you make a stand with your children, they are indeed angry at you, and may say you are unfair and mean-nobody enjoys being told he cannot have his way. But such outbursts are not enduring feelings or wisdom about real injustices. These outbursts are merely countermeasures to undermine parental authority. We need to clarify this and enable the parents to see them as such. We try to enable the parents to stand on a fair and reasonable position, and to avoid overestimating the significance of the youngsters' attempts to undermine them.

Our task then is to clarify that there are more effective alternatives and that, no, these alternatives do not get you into more trouble than you are in already. Reality therapy suggests as a major principle that we should not accept excuses. The suggestion here is to treat the excuses seriously, use them to troubleshoot the problems, and answer objections or adjust our programs to meet the objections.

It is essential as we clarify things to enable the clients to thoroughly accept and integrate the new understandings, and to maintain them so that they are continually available for use in their everyday lives. The next two sections focus on integrating and maintaining these understandings.

10
Instill New Patterns

1. Use illustrations and images.
2. Familiarize
3. Structure carry-over.

Use Illustrations and Images

Images and illustrations can construct critical distinctions in a way that entertains and intrigues the client, and so maintain rapport and avoid generating resistance.

Take the concept of avoidance motivation. Some actions are performed in order to get what you want, and others to avoid what you do not want. Avoidance motivations have two interesting characteristics: merely avoiding adversities is less satisfying than getting what you genuinely want, and seeking to avoid something can be readily confused with actually valuing its opposite. Avoidance motivations can be problematic, since they involve fewer satisfactions and are easily confused with strivings for things.

Poor No More. The following image introduces and clarifies some of the issues of avoidance motivation: "A middle-aged man comes into my office, and he is unsatisfied with his life. What matters to him most, as he tells it, is money. He is an executive and so makes a considerable amount of money, and he has all the accoutrements of the good life that money can buy. At this point, we want to say, `Wait a minute. If you care so much for money and you have so much of it, then why are you so unsatisfied?' We investigate further, and find that the fellow grew up dirt poor, humiliated and contemptuous of his poverty, and swore at an early age that he would not stay poor. He was smart enough and worked hard for many years, and so finds himself now with considerable money. Even though he has so much money, the possibility of poverty still frightens him, so he continues to struggle for more and more money, in order to avoid that possibility. So at this point, we know why he is so unsatisfied. It is not wealth that means something to him, but rather the avoidance of poverty. And running your whole life in order to avoid poverty cannot yield all that many satisfactions."

Poor No More can be applied to a variety of avoidance motivation problems. Consider for instance a young woman who is continually trying to please everyone and to avoid doing anything which might cause disapproval. She is outgoing and considerate, and indeed everyone does like her, or at least almost everyone. Yet life is unsatisfying; she lives in continual fear of others' opinions and does not enjoy the friendships which she does have. Her problem, as she sees it, is that she cares too much about others' approval.

Note first of all that there is something amiss in her assessment of her problem. She gets considerable approval from others, and if that were what she really cares about, she should find this satisfying and find herself feeling good about others instead of continually frightened by them. A better estimate is that what she mainly cares about is avoiding disapproval.

Poor No More can be used to introduce and structure consideration of such avoidance motivation issues in the following manner: "Your problem, as you see it, is that you care too much for others' approval. My impression, however, is that you do not really have your eye on the approval you are getting. My impression is that what you really care about is avoiding disapproval. Let me outline an image which we use to clarify these issues." The image is then presented to the client, and from there it is applied to the specific situation: "In your case, it is not poverty but rather disapproval which is of concern. It is not Poor No More but Unacceptable No More.

But the issues seem to be the same. You say you care too much about approval, but you have plenty of it, and if it really matters to you then why does it not make you happy? One answer is that it is not approval but avoiding disapproval which matters so much. Does that fit?" "This helps explain why you find so little satisfaction in the friendships you do have. When what matters is avoiding something, then the best that you can do is to break even: on a wrong day someone disapproves, while a perfect day is one in which you do not get any disapproval. Either way you do not get ahead, and there is little satisfaction."

Often the concept applies in some ways or to some extent, but does not apply in other ways. Perhaps the client strives to avoid disapproval from most acquaintances and from members of her family, but has a single close friend whose approval she sees and counts on. The image introduces the concept, and from there we confer with our clients on where and to what extent the distinction pertains. Where there are some areas of attainment motivations rather than avoidance motivations, then these provide an important contrast. The client can see that approval really can matter, and can use that to contrast and better understand the avoidance of disapproval.

The issue from here is to find ways for the avoidance of disapproval to become less significant as a life motivation. One way is to analyze directly the importance of the disapproval. How much disapproval is involved, and how much should it affect your life? A complementary approach is to suggest that gaining approval should be more important than the client allows it to be. The approval and love of others should give you satisfactions and build your esteem, so that as you gain good feelings from those who do approve, you are thereby fortified against times when someone disapproves. One who sees the problem as one of caring too much about approval has reason thereby to try to make approval matter less in her life, and that is what most persons have been doing who present the problem in these terms. Our therapeutic strategy then is to challenge directly the motivations to downgrade approval and to show the clients good reasons to upgrade it instead.

Avoidance motivations can take a variety of forms, and the image can be adapted to any of them. Poor No More became Unacceptable No More in the adaptation just discussed. One might strive to appear smart, sophisticated, or attractive but really care mainly about avoiding appearing stupid, graceless, or unattractive; one might strive to be popular and included but care mainly about avoiding being unpopular or lonely. A person might strive to win but care mainly about avoiding losing: It is not the sweetness of winning which is on the person's mind-it is avoiding the anguish of losing. The therapeutic image gives the sense of what is happening, how it might have come about, and what is wrong with a life constructed that way. It has implications for what to do to correct the problem.

An image plants the essential concepts in the mind of the client, and also serves to organize and hold the concept for us as therapists. Read over this image again, use it once or twice, and you should find it easy to catch avoidance motivation issues and to remember what to do about them. Will you ever hear another client say that he cares too much about others' approval without wondering if what he or she really cares about is avoiding disapproval? Some images are constructed for an individual client, while others are used over and over to present common issues with a variety of clients. Poor No More was suggested by Ossorio as a standard way to introduce avoidance motivations.

There is a natural sequencing of presenting and then applying imagery which works to our advantage. We present the image and elaborate on it so that the client understands the critical issues, and from there, we apply it to the client's situation. Presentation of the image itself is intriguing to most clients and invites them to ponder the issue before personally sensitive applications have been raised. It does not generate resistance, since it is about things in general rather than specific to the particular client. Once the image has been presented and the concept understood, it becomes easier from there to talk about where and to what extent it applies in the client's life.

Aphorisms, analogies, metaphors, mottoes, parables, poems, rules of thumb, stories, jokes, witticisms, and so on can all carry information. The use of any or all of these is appropriate to imprint information on clients' minds.

Several orientations are noted for using imagery and illustration, including modern Adlerians; adherents of transactional analysis; hypnotherapists in trance induction procedures, a la Milton Erickson; humanists, and advocates of guided fantasies. Imagery and illustration have been suggested recently to augment standard rational emotive procedures.[56] Many eclectics make liberal use of images and illustrations. It may be something of a neglected art nonetheless, for it is a complex skill, and there is too much emphasis in texts, journals, and training programs on condensing ideas, and too little attention is paid to bringing them to life. Writers frequently ignore the very stuff that makes information come alive, in the interest of saving space and perhaps also appearing serious minded. In clinical practice we have ample time to elaborate and embellish, and clients appreciate relief from the seriousness with which they too often conduct their own lives. The point is to communicate effectively so that clients see and maintain the ideas: for this images and illustrations are indispensable.

Familiarize

Surface understanding matters little, and new information must be more than merely heard and acknowledged to be of real benefit. It is essential that the client fully understand, accept, and integrate new viewpoints, and be able to apply them in everyday situations. The client must become familiar and comfortable with new understandings, and accomplished in recognizing when and where to apply them, and how they fit. As we clarify we give the client new ways to see and do things, and these must be used as a foundation for new competencies to see and act. Our objective is that the client gain the competency to apply new understandings in appropriate ways. To do this we have the client participate actively in the new viewpoints, and we go over new information as much and as thoroughly as is needed to understand and integrate it fully.

Try It On One excellent way to involve someone is to invite him to state aloud his apparent position or to rehearse a suggested position or action. Actually stating the position has more impact than merely hearing us interpret it for him. Suppose we discover that a young woman is showing her husband how much misery he has caused her in order to get him to see his responsibility and treat her better. Her operating premise is that showing he is causing her problems is a way to make him treat her better. We interpret this, and to bring it home, we have her say aloud to herself, "I am trying to make him recognize how miserable he is making me, in order to make him feel responsible so that he has to change." What does saying that bring forth in her? We ask, "Does it sound right to you?" Where it does sound right, the client is consciously recognizing an already existing operating position, is more involved, and is in a better position to reevaluate.

Involving someone more fully in his position corresponds to the Gestalt principle of having him "own" his position. Strategic therapy, in an interesting twist, has family members pretend the family symptoms in order to bring home the view that current patterns are an enactment.

Trying out alternatives is beneficial, for it enables the client to gain experience and confidence, and to identify with new ways of doing things. We support the person and approve of the actions, conveying that he is someone who does have the right to do that sort of thing and is doing reasonably well with it.

One advantage of having someone rehearse a new action in the session is that any problems or reservations he has about it become apparent quickly. The client tries out making a stand, for instance, and we ask, "How did it feel when you did that?" Perhaps it felt scary, awkward, or just plain rude. Problems with conducting the action readily become apparent, and we can attempt to correct them before they cause problems in everyday relationships. We must answer any reservations about alternative actions, for residual objections undermine confidence and lead to failures. Every now and then, on rare occasions, our suggested alternatives feel right on the first run-through.

There is considerable agreement that one should try on new ways of seeing oneself and new ways of acting even before it seems entirely comfortable or real to do so. Norman Vincent Peale's positive thinking approach suggests mentally visualizing one's objectives and believing you can accomplish them, and Maxwell Maltz's psychocybernetics suggests that seeing yourself as you wish to be guides your actions toward those objectives. Rehearsing alternative actions, often termed "behavioral rehearsal" and "role playing," is an integral part of behavioral and other active approaches. Adlerians suggest acting "as if" one agreed with a new position, and in a similar vein, Kelly's fixed role therapy suggests trying on new roles to form whole new identities. The "fake it until you can make it" slogan used in Alcoholics Anonymous has this same idea. Some use hypnotic trance states to encourage clients to become more and more comfortable with proposed changes. The rationale in all of these is that viewing and conducting oneself in a more constructive way help one to identify with and take over the better characteristics. Evidence that one who states a new position tends to change to agreement with that position is found in the social psychological research under "counter attitudinal acts." Trying on and practicing new views and new actions encourage comfortableness and identification with them, and make them one's own.

Cover It as Much as Is Needed. Commitments to existing views may be strong, and our new replacements must become familiar and practiced in order to overcome the old patterns and themselves become enduring. The amount of repetition required to establish and maintain new understandings can boggle the imagination. To really establish an idea, we present it, then often we need to go on to reiterate, answer objections, reiterate again, come at it from another angle, answer other objections or answer the same ones again, legitimize the problems the client is having in grasping it, introduce further supporting considerations, invite the client to make his own observations, restate the idea again, and so on. Considerable time and energy are often required to establish and maintain key understandings. The amount of repetition required is understandable when we consider how many years clients have held the old views and used them to structure their lives. The amount of repetition is justified when we recognize that key understandings can reorganize and alter for the better whole ways of life, and that in many cases easier shortcuts are simply not available.

Going over and over information requires of us as therapists considerable patience and comfort with the learning process others must go through to grasp something that is obvious to us, as well as some confidence that what we are suggesting is indeed important enough to be worth the trouble it takes to really get it across.

Behavioral orientations, because they grew up on the repetitiveness of the familiar conditioning paradigms, are notably strong on the use of repetition. Systematic desensitization alternates between imagining a stressful situation and relaxation, and several hours of repetition may be used to pair the situation to relaxation and calmness. Repetition is probably used in most active orientations much more than available writings suggest, for the repetitiveness of practice is not particularly fascinating and writings on the repetitiveness of practice are not particularly fascinating either. Case analyses giving the impression that a single therapeutic statement carries the day make more interesting literature, although single interventions seldom get us all that far in actual practice. So repetition remains a necessary, if not a necessarily intriguing, aspect of good psychotherapy practice. There is enough that is truly intriguing so that we should be genuinely thankful, and make the best of the repetition which is required of us.

The marked improvements in outlook from improved understandings may be quite transient: the new understandings must be maintained initially through continual vigilance; without continuing attention, they will give way to the older and more established patterns which they had replaced. One who learns to make stands may do so initially and have marked improvement in outlook, and then let the assertiveness issues slide as he goes on to other things and find himself with many of the same problems he had previously. One who is encouraged to grieve over a recent loss may feel markedly better-only to forget the lessons, stifle the grief process, and find himself with his previous confusions and fears. Solutions-even obvious and important ones-are not necessarily enduring, and issues that are solved once reemerge in the same forms requiring solution again. Issues once solved do not stay solved, and the note of caution here is to keep an eye out for those problems which we seem to have solved already. As a general principle: when problems reemerge, look first at the solutions which you put in place already and see that they remain in place; go on to other issues when you are satisfied that the previous basic solutions are still being used. The note of encouragement here is that the issues are much easier to clarify the second time, and we can point to the previous success to encourage the client for another go at it. The initial improvement indicates that we were on the right trail, and the relapse means only that we have not figured how to make it last. Some measures can be taken to promote carry-over of session gains and thus reduce the problems of relapses.

Structure Carry-over

Psychotherapy is often a special place-understanding, supportive, and insulated by four walls from the stresses of ongoing daily activities. It is in such an atmosphere that important advances are made: situations are safely explored, better understandings are acquired, and new directions are attained. Such gains, however, are initially tenuous, and may be easily forgotten as the client leaves the session and again becomes involved in the old patterns of his everyday life. Some special measures may be needed then to structure carry-over of acquired understandings into the client's day-to-day activities and relationships.

Make Notes. One obvious means of promoting carry-over is to write down important information covered in the session and give the notes to the client. Suggest that he review them on occasion in the intervening week or that he consider further some of the implications. The notes are generally appreciated, as they help the client to focus on the important points of the session. The notes give him something to hold on to. Many clients are concerned anyway about failing to remember the important issues, and having a record of the session allays these concerns.

Notes should be simple and should contain the major points agreed upon in the session. For example, a note might read: "I expect the worst from people, so I reject them before they can reject me." Considerable time might have been spent exploring that issue, and the note summarizes what has been agreed upon already. Notes may include something to ponder, as in the following variation: "I feel that if I stay away from other people, then I won't get hurt so much. So after all the time I've been avoiding others, why aren't I safe by now? Is my strategy going to work?" We may invite the client to keep his own journal of therapy insights and refer to it as he finds himself slipping back into old patterns.

Keeping notes for ourselves is a good learning aid for therapist trainees but seems less useful for experienced practitioners. Maintaining adequate records has been until recently an ethical responsibility, but various freedom of information rulings may jeopardize the confidentiality of such records. Many agencies require conscientious record keeping, while professionals with the freedoms of independent practice may rebel against note taking altogether, seeing it as uninteresting and an infringement on their time. The policy here of taking notes and giving them to our clients avoids the confidentiality problems, and introduces some new meaning into an old chore.

Include Family and Friends. Changes may be better maintained when family or friends are involved in the sessions. The companions may come to understand and accept our therapeutic interpretations and recommendations, help the client recognize unconstructive patterns when they occur, and encourage more constructive alternatives.

Standard crisis intervention for one who has lost a loved one and is suppressing the grief process is to encourage the client to allow himself to grieve freely. But such clients generally have the fears that if they start grieving, they will be unable to stop, and others who see them grieving will be upset by it or feel that they are coming unglued. Such fears are answered by reassurance that the grief process is not indefinite, and that others can and do understand bereavement. Perhaps we can enable the client to grieve more freely during the session, but on the outside there is less support, the old fears return, and the grief is again suppressed. We might instruct such a client to talk to his family or friends about the grief process and its importance, so that they can understand and be supportive of it. The alternative is to have family or friends in the actual sessions, so that communication is opened on these issues. Either way, the inclusion of significant others may be an essential support for the continuation of the grief process outside the actual sessions. When others are grieving the same losses, sharing can be especially helpful for everyone concerned.

Assign Activities. Understanding may be maintained through activities which force awareness of the important themes: with the mother who has as her premise that being upset should cause better conduct, we clarify and challenge her premise during the session. Nonetheless, the old pattern is an embedded one and should be expected to reassert itself outside the therapy session. How then would one promote the continuation of the insights into the family's everyday activities? The therapist involves mother and daughter in an activity-a game here-which incorporates the attained insights into a reconstructed version of the old pattern: "You see how the pattern is working so far. What we need is some means to continue this understanding into your day-to-day activities. Let's try a sort of game, which goes like this. Your task, Ms. Jones, is to try to control your daughter's misbehavior without becoming upset yourself. So, whenever you are able to exercise authority and maintain control, then you score one point for your side. And you, Julie, you need to provide your mother with some worthy competition. So, you try to get her upset, and whenever you manage to get her upset before she gets you to behave, then you score a point. You both keep track, and we'll see who has scored the most, points by next week. Okay?"

The assigned game thus rearranges the significance of the existing pattern. Until now the mother has counted being upset as an asset, since it should make the daughter behave. Now it counts openly as a loss. Now too the daughter's misbehavior counts openly as a fair and square tactic, which is exactly what it was for this youngster anyway. So the mother can hardly fail now to see it for what it is. In addition, since the daughter is generally oppositional, she may find it not so tempting or so satisfying to misbehave, because misbehavior now counts as compliance with agreed-upon instructions and not as straightforward opposition to parental authority. The scorecard is placed conspicuously on the refrigerator. On a day-to-day basis these two cannot continue to replay the old pattern without this continual reminder of what it is they are doing. The game thus structures the necessary insights into the family's everyday activities.

Review. In each session, we should follow up the major issues which were covered in the previous session and inquire about whether the client has thought about them further, whether or not they still make sense in the same way, and how he has done in applying them throughout the week. It is important for the client to expect to be asked about his progress with the material covered so that he has at least this incentive to do something with it now, rather than putting it off until that more convenient time which never comes.

When problems have been corrected and we are terminating therapy, it is often best to terminate gradually by spacing the sessions to every other week or to longer intervals. These intervals allow us to gauge how the clients do without the sessions and to monitor problems. In the initial phases of therapy, clients feel better during and after the sessions, but relapse later in the week as they lose sight of the new views and patterns which made things improve. We know that the new patterns we introduced have really taken hold and that therapy is nearly finished when clients make use of the new views and patterns during the week, and come to the next session feeling better for what they have accomplished on their own.

Various tasks and activities are assigned to structure carry-over in active approaches including behavioral, cognitive, rational-emotive, and reality therapies. Activities with a paradoxical twist, such as the game just discussed, are typical of communications and family systems interventions.

11

Motivations

Make use of whatever interests and values the client already has, rather than ignoring or trying to oppose them.

Appeal to what matters.
Avoid generating resistance.

Appeal to What Matters

Any interpretation or suggestion should appeal to something which matters to the client, so that he has motivation to accept and utilize the intervention rather than to ignore or resist it. Motivations for specific actions arise from the individual's more general interests and values as applied to the immediate situation. We need to appeal to those existing interests and values to motivate changes, so that the person sees the suggested action as a way of getting something which matters to him.

General interests and values do change, but quite slowly, so that rapid motivational changes are best made by appealing to those values which already exist. We should present what the client needs to see and do in ways that make use of, rather than challenge, what already matters to him.

Note the appeal is to what matters to the client, not what matters most to us or what should matter to the client. It is easy to attribute solid priorities to clients who have no such thing.

The guidelines in the previous chapters all involved implicit appeals to what matters to the clients. As clarify operating premises, we show that the means the client is using cannot get for him what he is motivated to attain. When he becomes convinced that particular actions do not get him what he is after, he loses his reasons to continue. As we generate alternatives, we must show that they are appropriate and effective means to obtain what the client wants, so that she has reason to use them to get what matters to him. Note that we do not try to legislate what should or ought to matter, but focus on what does matter to the individual client.

Clients seize eagerly upon suggestions which they see as practical ways to get what genuinely does matter to them. Suggestions which appeal to what ethically or normatively should matter, but not to what really does matter, are ignored or resisted, and fail to promote changes. Indeed, an excellent means to see what does matter is to appeal to an expected motivational priority and see whether the client responds positively on the basis of those motivations, or whether she ignores or resists the appeal. When a client remains unenthusiastic about a practical means to do something we expected would matter to him, we should reevaluate whether his priorities are as we had expected.

To a mother who values her children's spontaneity but cares little for propriety and social conventions, we might suggest that structuring things more would improve the children's relationships with others and so leave them freer to be themselves. With one who values propriety and cares little about the inner lives of her children, we might take the opposite tack and suggest that giving them some freedom and accepting more playfulness would make the children calmer and better adjusted, so that they would fit in better and cause fewer social problems. Each program has its validity, and each is an attempt to appeal to the concerns of the parent. Were we to argue the importance of a program to increase children's freedom and spontaneity to the mother who values propriety above all, it would come to naught. She would be too worried about how these free and spontaneous children would fit in, and what sorts of embarrassments they would cause her by their inappropriate actions.

We may occasionally succeed by merely instructing a client to do something, for our authority and status as therapists do provide some reason to comply with our instructions. But reliance merely on authority wears thin, because many clients have other priorities and are not particularly interested in following instructions which they do not see as clear solutions. It is better to give the rationale and have a client see the objectives she might gain by taking the suggestion. Our clients, like everyone else, are better motivated when they see how the programs are going to gain them something they care about.

Our task is to show the clients that by making changes, they attain what matters to them and do not lose something else in the process. When they see sufficient reasons to change their actions, they change -and not merely because we have suggested, instructed, or ordered them to: they change because they see more clearly the reasons for and against an action, and see it as a way of getting what genuinely matters to them. So it is not a matter of making suggestions and then struggling to get our clients to comply with them. We clarify the reasons for a change, show how it might be done, and must rely on their existing interests and values to provide the motivation.

Formal written contracts may be used to make things explicit and to structure carry-over of the agreements into daily activities, but they do not really increase the clients' motivations to comply with the program. Those who are not sufficiently motivated before contracting remain insufficiently motivated after signing the contract, and fail to comply with the program. Such failures to comply can be extremely frustrating for therapists who are too strongly committed to the agreed-upon contracts: after all, they agreed to do it, it is here in black and white, and then they reneged on their agreements. It is too tempting, but notoriously unproductive, to hold the clients solely responsible and to require them to uphold their agreements before therapy can proceed. Contract or no contract, the same considerations hold: when the clients see sufficient reason, they comply; when they do not see sufficient reason, they do not comply. When contracts are broken, it is because the clients do not see sufficient reasons for compliance or have stronger reasons against it. Our task as therapists is to reevaluate the issues. If the contracted program does not appeal sufficiently to existing interests and values, it needs to be rewritten.

Consider emancipation issues so often encountered by young adults in their attempts to reconcile steps toward independence with parents who expect to maintain things as they have been. One university student is troubled by his relationship with his mother, who presents herself as generally miserable, complains that he does not telephone or visit her enough, and argues that he is ungrateful and does not love her. The young man feels obligated, inadequate, and trapped by the seemingly endless problems. He encourages his mother to find other friends and other interests, but she offers "yes but" excuses and continues to complain. His mother expects her children to stay with her, and through her misery and accusation she compels compliance with her expectations.

The young man seeks independence, but he also feels very responsible, wants to do what is right for his mother, and is wary of being the cause of even more unhappiness. He is being adversely affected by the essentially manipulative tactics his mother is using, and one important step is to clarify the manipulativeness. Perhaps that can yield some progress, although his concern for his mother runs deep and impedes his attempts toward independence.

One might suggest that he should look out for himself more and let his mother take care of herself, but that would run counter to something that matters considerably to him: acting responsibly matters a great deal, and ignoring mother seems quite irresponsible. A better strategy is one which attempts to incorporate, rather than to challenge or bypass, his sense of responsibility. An example of this follows.

We mention that compliance with emotional manipulation impedes any genuine solution, for compliance only satisfies and encourages further manipulation: "You are extremely concerned about your mother, but is your compliance with her emotional coercion the right thing to do? She has learned that by being miserable enough and blaming you she will force you to come to the rescue. If she solved her problems herself, she would ruin her case, so she has no incentive to do that and she is not trying to make the best of things for herself. Instead, she indulges in her miseries, for that has the desired effect of obligating and binding you to her. Whenever you comply, you strengthen the pattern because you confirm for your mother that unhappiness is the way to obligate you.

"Your intention through your compliance has been to make your mom feel better, but has it actually achieved your aims?" The conclusion here must be that, no, the mother is not getting better and may be actually getting worse. "Compliance may be the easiest thing at the moment, but if you really do want to help your mother with her emotional problems, then you will need to attempt something which has some real chance of working. Is it worth a try?" We get an agreement by the client to consider an alternative.

"You will need to avoid complying with your mother's upsetness and emotional intimidation, for only when emotional manipulation is no longer working will she be free to seek some more constructive alternatives. Let's look at some alternate responses you might make, rehearse and practice them, and see how they would feel."

Compliance with the manipulation is presented here as the too easy quick fix, while resisting the manipulation is the only really responsible course of action. If the student continues to worry that he should be taking more responsibility for mother's unhappiness, then the groundwork has been laid: "You may feel guilty in your conversations with your mother, but that does not mean that you are guilty. Your mom uses unhappiness to manipulate and obligate, and in opposing that tactic you already are acting responsibly and doing the right thing. In the long run, this will actually help your mother." It is no longer an issue of independence versus responsibility, but rather of integrating independence and responsibility into a viable way of life. Responsibility matters to this individual, and appeals to responsibility are used here to justify and to encourage his independence.

The appeal to existing motivations has been presented by Miller and Rollnick, in motivational interviewing, which clarifies healthy motivations over troublesome ones.57

Poisoning the Well

Some actions involve motivations which are incompatible with other more general values, but the actions occur nonetheless because the actor remains unaware of his own motivations and fails to see the implicit contradiction. By pointing out these motivations, we appeal to his more important values and show the person that he has reasons to not continue the action.

A person who abhors the competitive pursuit of status may nonetheless stay aloof from others as a way of showing himself to be superior to them; one who fears harming others may sulk as a camouflaged way of getting even; one who genuinely loves her child may be too harsh on him in public to show other parents that she is not playing favorites. Such motivations continue unrecognized in contradiction to the individual's stronger and more general values. Interpreting such motivations calls attention to them and allows the client to see the contradiction. With one who values cooperation, we might comment: "By staying aloof from others, you present yourself as someone who is so superior that you are not even concerned with social recognition. When you consider it, that is quite some status claim in itself." If the person really does value cooperation and abhor competetiveness, then he has reason to give up his aloofness.

Motives which are in contradiction to more general values are hard for clients to acknowledge and accept. Our interpretations of these may involve some struggle and conflict, although in the context of a sufficiently strong therapeutic alliance we can get clients to accept them. Once the interpretation has been accepted, the previous satisfactions are ruined, and the clients have reason to not continue the action and are forced to look in other directions for alternative satisfactions. Such interpretations are termed "poisoning the well" by Ossorio and "spitting in the soup" by Adler. In both images it takes only a small dose of this to ruin what had been a reservoir of satisfaction.

For such interpretations to work, it is essential that the more general values really do matter. Sometimes we can be fooled, for most people want to appear to be loving and committed even when they are really not that way. A young woman who cares about propriety, status, and security would want to appear to be good and loving to her sweetheart, even if she has little interest in those things which would genuinely benefit him. Pointing out that she is angry and acting to obligate and subordinate him would annoy and embarrass her, and perhaps invite her to feel guilty, but it would not cause her to be more generous toward him. Interpreting improper intentions evokes changes only when it genuinely matters more to be individual to be another sort of way. With this woman it would be better to focus on and legitimize the anger and insecurity, and to avoid mentioning her professed commitment to being a loving companion.

"Games" interpretations in transactional analysis seek leverage by showing the manipulative aspects of the actions. If it matters sufficiently to the client to avoid those manipulations, then such interpretations spoil the satisfactions and give reasons to stop the manipulative actions. If it does not matter enough to change, then such interpretations may be mildly annoying or entirely unacceptable, and they are too soon forgotten.

Mining the Gold.

Everyone is familiar with denial and rationalization, in which improper motives go unrecognized. As surprising as it might seem, many persons have good motives and fail to recognize the altruistic or noble aspects of their actions. Afraid of rationalizing, these persons deceive themselves instead by failing to see that which is genuinely good about themselves. They cheat themselves out of the confidence and satisfactions they should have earned by their actions, and weaken their reasons to continue those actions. By interpreting the good motives which do exist, we accredit the person as one of good character and also bring those positive values to bear to maintain or increase the beneficial actions. One might be genuinely concerned about a friend and act to protect him, but not want to be conspicuous and so shrug it off as merely meddlesomeness or idle curiosity. By interpreting for the clients their correct motives, we accredit and also strengthen the reasons they have to continue with those sorts of actions.

There is a popular misconception in our field that it is the clients' responsibility to be already motivated to make particular changes and that until they are so motivated they cannot progress in therapy. A recent joke asks, "How many psychiatrists does it take to change a light bulb?" The answer is "Only one, but it takes a long time and the light bulb has to really want to change." Motivation is certainly essential to therapeutic change, but it is not essential that clients come already motivated to undertake whatever programs a therapist is prone to suggest. Clients come with their own motivations, and it should be our responsibility as therapists to present programs for change which appeal to whatever motivations they already have. Clients are motivated to change as they become convinced that such changes are ways to gain what matters to them without losing in the process; they are not motivated to change when they see losses rather than advantages in such changes.

Behavior modification suggests explicit appeals to what matters: it assesses what matters to the client under the cover term "reinforcers" and then uses those things as incentives for behavior changes. Behavior consultants structure situational contingencies so that the person must follow the program in order to get something she values. Other orientations are more implicit in their appeals to what matters, but all effective intervention must appeal to what matters. Logo (meaning) therapist Victor Frankl (1963) appeals to what matters in the following sensitive comments:

Once, an elderly general practitioner consulted me because of his severe depression. He could not overcome the loss of his wife, who had died two years before, and whom he had loved above all else. Now how could I help him? What should I tell him? I ... confronted him with the question, "What would have happened, Doctor, if you had died first, and your wife would have had to survive you?" "Oh," he said, "for her this would have been terrible; how she would have suffered!" Whereupon I replied, "You see, Doctor, such suffering has been spared her, and it is you who have spared her this suffering; but now you have to pay for it by surviving and mourning her." (pp. 178-179)

The comments clarify the possible significance of the suffering. The intervention appeals to the physician's love for his wife, so that his continuance of an otherwise empty life may attain a completeness now as a final expression of endearment and commitment to his beloved. "Suffering," comments Frankl, "ceases to be [merely] suffering ... at the moment it finds a meaning, such as the meaning of a sacrifice" (p. 179). The intervention has the effect it does because it appeals to an important and already existing commitment: it would be lost on an individual who was less altruistic.

Avoid Generating Resistance.

"[Psychotherapy involves] a series of therapeutic thrusts and parries, ... in an effort to dissolve, to avoid, or to take advantage of, rather than to break down, resistance. Consequently, therapy ... follows the rule of least resistance in an effort to bring about therapeutic changes..."

An "old saying" has it that resistance is the second oldest form of human interaction ever conducted: when the first person suggested doing something, somebody else said no. While this is perhaps an overstatement, it suggests an

187

important warning: resistance is an integral aspect of human nature which, unless carefully monitored, can attain an exaggerated importance, frustrating therapist and client alike by undermining the therapeutic alliance, overshadowing cooperative motivations, and so interfering with attempts to deal with anything more constructive.

Not every therapeutic failure should be taken as an indication of resistance, however. A client who does not accept an interpretation may be limited by his idiosyncratic concepts, misunderstandings, or insecurities, and not merely resisting the interpretation. One who does not comply because she is not capable of following the suggestion need not be resisting the suggestion; nor is one resisting who does not comply because she fails to see sufficient reasons to do so. A client who fails to understand an interpretation may be merely unable to understand and not necessarily resisting, just as one who fails to make a suggested stand with his boss may be genuinely fearful of the consequences and not merely resisting the therapist. Every failure to comply is not the result of resistance.

It is especially important to carefully delineate our concept of resistance, so that problems resulting from authentic resistance can be identified and distinguished from other problems, and treated accordingly. Resistance, as the term is used here, is active or passive opposition to something, and not merely confusion, lethargy, or inertia. It is a purposive action which is conducted for intelligible reasons and not merely an inadvertent failure to act. What is it that one perceives which gives him intelligible reason to resist? The situation as perceived has two aspects: it is seen as a force-an authority, power, or pressure to comply-and as unfair-as callous, intrusive, threatening, or otherwise unwarranted and unjust. These two together provide reason to resist: that which is resisted must be seen as force or pressure, for otherwise there would be nothing to resist; the force must be seen as unfair or unwarranted, for otherwise there would be no reason to resist and one would comply instead. The term "coercion" ordinarily refers to a force which is unjust; and is used in this sense here. Therefore, the occurrence of resistance indicates that the client perceives something as coercive.

Some obvious and unambiguous cases might help represent the concept. Resistance may be active opposition, as in the French resistance to German occupation, or passive opposition, as in Gandhi's "passive" resistance to British rule in India. Either way, it is something seen as coercion which gives one reason to resist, and the resistance is actual opposition and not merely inertia. The concept of resistance outlined here includes one major ordinary language meaning of the term but is more tightly restrictive than familiar psychiatric usage. Our use of the term specifically excludes merely withstanding something and is used only to indicate opposition.

The clarification is important, for it enables us to distinguish between quite separate varieties of noncompliance too often grouped together indiscriminately under the same cover term. Therapeutic failures resulting from various confusions and inadequacies, or to happenstance are not to be considered resistance. The client who is merely afraid of making a suggested assertive stance or who gets caught in unexpected traffic and arrives late for his appointment is not seen as resisting therapy.

A therapist who encounters instances of noncompliance such as these and routinely interprets them as resistance is going to have a peculiar effect on the client. Most clients would feel misunderstood, and perhaps mistreated and manipulated, and would oppose and resist the interpretations. Inappropriate interpretations of resistance are seen as coercive, evoke resistance, and so become self-fulfilling prophecies. To avoid generating resistance, a first principle is to avoid interpreting and thus creating resistance when it does not occur naturally on its own.

The distinction between opposition and confusion, incompetence, or mere inertia is important in choosing a course of action. When a client merely fails to understand or to accept an interpretation, we are free to pursue our case-to mention supporting information, to reiterate or rephrase the point, to use illustrations, and so on. Considerable support for an interpretation and reiteration may be necessary to familiarize the client with the information and enable him to use it himself, as suggested by earlier guidelines. But when a client is actually

resisting an interpretation, further support generally evokes only further resistance, so we are advised to troubleshoot the resistance rather than to press the argument. Being able to tell the difference is essential to our course of interventions.

The occurrence of resistance is minimized by conscientious adherence to many of the earlier guidelines: maintaining a collaborative alliance, legitimizing and making acceptable the client's actions, appealing to what genuinely matters to the client, and so on. Nonetheless, some client resistance seems unavoidable, for in a course of interventions there is generally something objectionable, and there are of course those clients who feel oppressed by life itself and so are predisposed to resist anything that might be suggested.

When resistance does occur, we troubleshoot the problem using the ` concept that something perceived as coercion is giving the client reason to resist. Our initial task is to find out what aspect of the relationship the client sees as coercive, and why. Such troubleshooting often yields readily apparent solutions: one woman feels slighted by a friend whom she then undermines and subtly antagonizes. An interpretation to this client of her hostility meets with resistance, and attempts to show her the indications of her anger only generate further resistance. As sometimes occurs with anger interpretations, the focus on the hostility exposes the woman's own participation in the antagonism, which she sees not as assistance but rather as an indictment of her own position. She sees the interpretation of her anger as coercive. Continuation of the interpretation should be avoided, to avoid generating further resistance, and alternate means should be sought for dealing with the issue.

Resistance to an interpretation may be minimized by omitting that aspect of the interpretation which is objectionable. When the intentions are unacceptable, a client might nonetheless accept an interpretation of his behavior in the form of a behavior outcome description, in which intentions are specifically omitted. With the woman who undermines and subtly antagonizes a friend, we are well advised to begin with an outcome description, such as: "Your comments might seem to be ignoring or contradicting your friend quite a bit, and she is being antagonized by them." If she objects to the interpretation and argues that this is not what she is doing, or is not what she means to do, then there is room to more explicitly limit the thrust: "I'm not saying that you necessarily mean to antagonize her, but only that when you say those sorts of things, it has that sort of effect." The outcome, that the friend is antagonized, is obvious anyway. Since the interpretation omits the intention, it is not seen as an indictment and there is no reason to resist.

Although intentions are not here in play, a behavior outcome description does carry with it its own force and leverage. When one acknowledges that an action causes an outcome, whether intentionally or inadvertently, she thereby attains some reason to change the action if he wants to change the outcome: "Even though you may not mean to antagonize her, it has that effect. You have reason to make some changes if it matters enough to you to avoid further problems there."

Sometimes peculiar or unusual factors are involved. A young man has progressed from a mental breakdown to a level of at least minimal functioning, and the therapist comments that he might expect further progress and might even come to enjoy himself sometimes. Although the comment appears promising and supportive, the client resists, and any attempts to further support the good prognosis generate further resistance. The fellow argues that he is as well as he is ever going to be and, to further his point, suggests terminating therapy. In the absence yet of sufficient understanding, we should retract the prognosis to alleviate the resistance and reestablish an alliance, and should seek to understand the cause of the puzzling client reaction. Further inquiry reveals that the young man is closely involved with his mother, that each claims various infirmities and disabilities, and that by convention, the healthier one is morally obligated to care for and cater to the needs and complaints of the "sicker" one. To this individual, the significance of the positive prognosis is that he is again to be responsible for his mother, and the suggestion that he work for that is understandably seen as coercive.

The additional information provides the basis for a more acceptable intervention: "If you do get better, then you will feel obligated to take care of your mother and to struggle with her continual unhappiness, complaints, and accusations. Is she really all that ill, though, or is she merely appearing so miserable to manipulate you into feeling obligated and doing what she directs? Let's look into it, shall we? For now, though, there is no point in becoming healthy just yet if by doing so you have to give up your freedom and your happiness."

Clients resistance does impede progress in therapy, but we should not conclude therefore that anyone values sickness. In the case just discussed, resisting therapy was the means used, and maintaining freedom from filial obligations was the significance of the action. Clients do not resist therapy merely to stay sick, but rather for some further and more understandable aims. Consideration of those more sensible reasons is a source of more appropriate and effective therapeutic interventions.

Resistance may be interpreted directly, although the approach is extremely important. "You are being resistive" would be an ineffective comment, for if the client is feeling mistreated already he would tend to see that as further accusation. Embellishments on the theme, such as "You are resisting seeing things as they really are" or "You are resisting getting well," would only make matters worse, for they offer the same accusation but with additional punch. They tend to engender further resistance. Legitimizing the resistance can offer the needed entree, for example: "It may feel as though I'm trying to push you into seeing it my way and I'm not listening enough to what you have to say." This could be expressed in a slightly different form: "You're not the sort of person who is going to let someone else tell him what to do. You don't like it when others tell you what to do, and you don't like it when I tell you what to do. I realize that, and I see now that you need more room to make you own choices." We thus accept the client's position and agree to alter somewhat the directiveness which the client finds objectionable.

Clients may have vested interests which we should be well aware of before we begin a crusade. Mistaken attitudes and ideologies need to be challenged, but we should be aware of where our clients stand and of the extensiveness of their commitments. As a reminder: When you go out to slay a dragon, make sure it is not somebody's pet. When resistance does occur, look at the commitments the client has and tread lightly on favored icons.

The present ordinary language concept of resistance was clarified by Ossorio in his formal descriptive psychology concepts. A social psychological approach uses a concept of resistance similar to the present one but labels it "reactance" (of. Brehm, 1976). The present formulation contrasts of course with the classical analytic formulations which focus exclusively on intrapsychic mechanisms and overlook the contributions of situations and relationship factors. As a general principle: When resistance occurs, assess what you are doing which is seen by the client as coercive, and then alter or avoid it, in order to maintain a cooperative relationship in which issues can be dealt with productively.

Exceptions/ In some situations, we may choose to take advantage of resistance rather than try to avoid generating it. We might suggest that the client continue or even accelerate a troublesome pattern, but now with an awareness of his actions and of his reasons for the actions. The rationale may be that he needs to become consciously familiar with the troublesome tendency in order to gain fuller understanding and conscious control in the matter. But if the action is something which is already annoying, the suggestion to continue or even accelerate the pace will be especially obnoxious. Notice here it is the suggestion which is to be resisted, not the therapist or the relationship. The client should know full well that the therapist wants him to overcome his futile tendencies and is only instructing that he continue with them for his own best interest. The technique involves "paradoxical intention," since the apparent intention is to continue the troublesome action and the effect is that the client stops.

One who pressures himself continually to force himself to improve may instead frustrate and exhaust himself. His operating premise is that more pressure should cause improvement; our objective after clarifying his premise is to help him convince himself that it is invalid and so lessen his use of pressure for self-improvement. When the client is firmly committed to his approach, we may invite him to continue pressuring himself as long as he wishes and thus to invalidate the approach for himself: "Perhaps being tough on yourself is the golden road to improvement, and you just haven't yet given it a fair chance. You might want to try it for a few more days or a few more weeks or months, or you might try being even tougher on yourself. In any case, when you are being tough on yourself, say to yourself, `I'm going to really force myself to really improve.' Then go at it with a vengeance." The pressure the client puts on himself has always been uncomfortable, and the conscious execution of even greater pressure should become exceptionally coercive. The client comes to resent the whole approach to self-improvement, but to actually resist the directive he must discontinue the pressure he puts on himself, which is of course the point of the exercise. As he follows the program he is learning a valuable lesson, and as he sees the good reasons to resist the program he is cured.

We may instruct the client who is generally resistive and oppositional to continue a troublesome activity, so that

194

continuing the activity counts as compliance with the instructions. It is an appeal to what already matters, and if it matters enough to resist our instructions, then to do so one must discontinue the problem activity. This principle was applied in an earlier illustration in which a resistive teenager was instructed to challenge her mother's authority. Should she continue to challenge as she had been doing, she would be cooperating with our therapeutic program, but she must stop challenging her mother to resist the instruction.

A second illustration involves a mother's catering to her youngest son Tommy, now a young adult, to the detriment of both. The arrangement provides Tommy's necessities and finances alcohol, narcotics, and stagnation. The mother stays an emotional wreck. The family prevails on her over and over to put Tommy on his own, but she will have none of it. She had been forced too many times to comply with her husband's orders, and with him now deceased, she is unwilling to give in anymore. What matters to this woman is independence and control over her activities, and she is willing to resist anyone and everyone to maintain it.

The family naturally assumes that their mother should value her son's welfare and her own peace of mind as well, but in appealing to these considerations they merely frustrate themselves. The impasse is best solved by appealing not to what should matter, but rather to what actually does matter. We advise an older brother who consults us to send a notice to all the family members, and a copy to mother as well, that they should stop interfering in their mother's affairs. He argues in the letter that mother and Tommy are ideally suited for each other: Mom is growing older, she will need companionship and someone to look after her as advancing age diminishes her spirit and capacities, and dims her judgment. And Tommy, despite his shortcomings, is the only one in the family with the patience and temperament for the difficult task ahead.

Everyone is appalled by the uninvited intrusion, and the mother responds by reversing her course and forcing Tommy out on his own, where he falters initially but might grab hold when faced with the stark necessities. Why does the intrusive intervention have this paradoxical

effect? Mother is not about to take orders from anybody, and she is not about to accept her suggested status as a deteriorating geriatric. What matters most dearly to her is maintaining control, and to resist the intrusion and maintain her independence, she is even willing to move out her younger son who is, after all, less competent than she. By seeming to force mother and by presenting her as a potential incompetent, the letter appeals in a backward way to what actually does matter. Paradoxical interventions such as these are a main staple in several family systems approaches.

The critical problem with a paradoxical intervention such as this is that it is altogether too appealing. The tactic is manipulative, for it involves fooling people to cause them to act in their own best interests. Also, it is a risky gambit, for the tactician is inviting the subject to tell him to go to hell and, in so doing, to change what that person needs to change. If it fails, the damage has been done, and there are fewer options for further interventions. Note that in the case just discussed, the paradoxical appeal to resistance was used by the brother to intervene in a family where cooperation mattered little and the other family members had no interest in changing. The manipulative tactic can be justified here since the family was stubborn and intransigent, there was no therapeutic relationship to rely on or jeopardize between the man writing the letter and his mother or younger brother, and straightforward non-manipulative appeals had proved to be failures.

In this case, the therapist acted as a collaborator in explaining the intervention and advising the brother to try it out. Manipulative interventions such as this might be used directly on the clients themselves, but such tactics have limited utility and carry with them strong cautions. The use of manipulative tactics on clients can sacrifice an already fragile alliance, undermine our credibility and, when they fail, further restrict our options for more cooperative interventions. Clients generally have some interest in changing, and a wide range of more cooperative means is available to promote those changes. The recommendation here is that we avoid treating clients with tactics which are manipulative and which appeal solely to resistance, except when no therapeutic relationship can be established and when opposition is the only available motivation we can use for change. In general, we do considerably better by maintaining a cooperative alliance with our clients, maintaining credibility in ourselves and our programs, clarifying for the clients how the programs will get for them what they want, and appealing to interests and values other than opposition and resistance.

12
Synthesis

The guidelines cover the range of major therapeutic objectives, and we must select the ones which are important in any specific situation. Some are critical across sessions, while others pertain to circumscribed issues. Relationship guidelines are implemented across sessions, but in the pursuit of other objectives and with minimum precautions unless problems occur, and then they receive our full attention. Accreditation guidelines find their way into every issue. Assessment occurs throughout the sessions, and things are reassessed when expected progress fails to materialize. The clarification guidelines are used when there may be ambiguities and confusions about things-which means they are included in almost every issue imaginable. Clarifying what is so and how to change things is at the heart of therapy, and the other guidelines set the stage for these objectives. The motivation guidelines find their way into any attempt to promote changes.

Many of the guidelines are interrelated, so that by going after one objective we usually attain several more as well. Really good interventions may accomplish several related objectives. A statement which legitimizes may thereby make things more acceptable, maintain the alliance, maintain our credibility, appeal to what matters, confirm the client's control, and when the client agrees, it may help confirm our initial assessment of the problem.

In some cases, one guideline objective must be balanced against other objectives so that nothing is sacrificed. When we confirm his control with the client invested in being the victim, we risk antagonizing, so we must ease the thrust with other components which legitimize and make the interpretation more acceptable. When we clarify things and push alternatives too strongly, we risk leaving the client behind, so we must balance these moves by understanding any reluctance the client has and by accepting and legitimizing it. The guidelines overlap and complement each other. Covering the spectrum of critical objectives and techniques, they work together in a single integrated approach to psychotherapy.

Considerable sensitivity and clinical judgment may be involved in weighing which of the guidelines pertain in any specific situation and in figuring out what to say to accomplish those objectives. The application of the guidelines becomes easier as one becomes more familiar with them and gains experience using them in clinical practice. There is always room to improve, by figuring out better and faster ways of attaining various therapeutic objectives and by finding better ways to coordinate the objectives with each other. The guidelines serve to guide and assist us in constructing appropriate and sometimes innovative interventions well suited to the particular situations we encounter, but they cannot tell us what will be appropriate in every particular situation. The guidelines should augment and assist our sensitivity and clinical judgment, but not replace it.

The guidelines contain both broad therapeutic objectives and some techniques which are suggested as ways to attain the objectives. The objectives should be recognized by most eclectic psychotherapists as sensible and important aspects of therapeutic practice. The guidelines are used to organize and make sense of the wide variety of familiar therapeutic techniques, which are seen as ways of attaining one or more of the guideline objectives. In many cases, techniques from one orientation may be more appropriate in some situations and those from another orientation more appropriate in other situations. In some cases, techniques from one orientation are seen as preferred ways of attaining an objective, and techniques from other orientations are judged poor by comparison. Other practitioners may have slightly different impressions, and there are undoubtedly some techniques favored by some which were considered here as poor or simply omitted. Considerable personal judgment has been involved in selecting and integrating the techniques to the guideline objectives, and there is room here for questions, alterations, and improvements. The set of guidelines is suggested as an initial framework for a comprehensive eclecticism, but not as a final or complete coverage of all aspects of eclectic practice.

The guidelines can be used to look at any intervention, for any specific intervention or general technique can be rated by independent practitioners as to what it would tend to accomplish in which sorts of situations. Similarly, these guidelines can be used to judge other orientations, for they can be rated on how well they tend to accomplish each of the guideline objectives. The guidelines provide a grid for understanding, organizing, and evaluating the vast array of therapeutic techniques.

When therapy is not going well, chances are that we are overlooking one or more of the guidelines. Check out your cheat sheet, and see if something is missing.

The use of physiological agents, when appropriate, must be coordinated with the psychological interventions suggested by the guidelines. As psychotherapists, it is our job to be alert to indications for physiological treatments and to refer for medication, nutritional advice, and so on. It also usually falls on us to address objections and convince the clients that an appropriate regimen of medication is indeed good for them, or that fewer calories or more exercise is really possible. The actions of medications or nutritional changes are physiological, but getting the clients to comply belongs in our realm of psychological interventions.

Outline of Guidelines

Guidelines are prescriptions for action based on considerations of our objectives, and of the principles and ways by which we might best achieve those objectives. The guidelines are general enough to apply across cases and to a wide range of problems. Proper application of these guidelines yields immediate tactical advantage and over the long run should markedly improve our effectiveness as therapists.

Outline of Guidelines[58]

I. The Therapeutic Relationship

1. Be Respectful. Act in the best interest of the client. Be committed, and avoid or resolve attitudes and feelings which interfere.

2. Maintain an Alliance. Act to enable the client to see you as an ally. Begin where you are welcome. Be personable and active, correct misunderstandings, and counter transference.

3. Stay Credible. Show the sense of what you are doing, and relate improvements to the contributing therapeutic procedures. Avoid statements which are untrue, and be careful with those which appear naive or false to the client.

4. Communicate an Understanding of the Client's Position. Share your impressions of the client's feelings and concerns.

5. Share Responsibility for Improvement. Take responsibility in ways which enable the client to better take responsibility. Provide what the client is unable herself to provide, and encourage her to do what she is able to do. Tailor interventions to the client's capacities to learn.

II. Affirmation and Accreditation

Accredit existing strengths. Treat the client as one who already makes sense, is acceptable, and is in control. Clients underestimate themselves, and acknowledging existing strengths is an essential step to using those strengths to better advantage.

1. Legitimize (Show the Client the Sense She Makes).Any of the everyday explanatory concepts can make sense of existing experiences and actions. Misunderstandings or unusual reasons may make sense of puzzling actions; unusual situations or individual characteristics make sense of those reasons; and personal learning experiences may make sense of confusing individual characteristics.

2. Make It Acceptable. Decriminalize. Interpret your client's characteristics in ways she can accept. Create a comfortable atmosphere. Use humor. Select acceptable phrasings. Emphasize positives; underplay negatives. Introduce norms.

3. Confirm the Client's Control. See the client as someone who is already in control of his actions. Show the reasons she has for the ways she controls. Show the ways she is successful.

4. Don't Buy Victim Acts. A client may present himself as a victim in order to avoid responsibility or to gain sympathy. Interpret and legitimize the reasons for the act. Challenge the ideology which affords special sympathy and privileges to the sufferer.

5. If It Works, Don't Fix It. See strengths as strengths. Avoid introducing uncertainties into areas which are already appropriate and functional.

III. Assessment

1. Assess What Matters. Assess what is needed for effective intervention, including problematic characteristics and also strengths. Most important are those factors which contribute significantly to the overall problems and which can be altered most readily by intervention. Stay with specifics. Omit extraneous information.

2. Use Ordinary Language Concepts. Use norms for points of reference, and avoid explanations which are too general. Recognize what the client means by the words he uses.

3. Collaborate. Ask for particulars. Outline plausible interpretations, and collaborate on which ones apply. Monitor judgment. Recreate key episodes; invite interactions with family or friends.

4. Learn As You Go. Interweave assessment and intervention. Intervene, and learn from the clients' reactions. Successes may confirm initial assessments; use failures to further understand the problems. Begin with the simplest adequate interpretations, and elaborate as additional leverage is needed.

5. Don't Expect the Client to Be Somebody Else. Realize that problems are often entrenched and may survive your initial or most obvious solutions. Avoid holding the client responsible for that which she is unable to do.

IV. Clarifications
Address inabilities to understand what is happening.
1. Clarify Situations. Address errors, and suggest clearer views of the real world. Weigh alternatives with the client, and encourage the client to observe for himself. Legitimize misunderstandings. Emphasize understandings over misunderstandings.
2. Clarify Concepts. Introduce and apply distinctions which the client can use himself. Build upon existing ordinary language concepts. Elaborate impoverished concepts. Untangle confounded concepts.
3. Deal with the Reality Basis of Emotions. Fear and anxiety are related to perceived threat or danger; anger, to provocation; guilt, to wrongdoing. Deal constructively with the circumstances generating the emotion and not merely with the experience or feeling.

V. Ways and Means
1. Clarify Misunderstandings How (Operating Premises). Look at the means by which the client is trying to get what she wants. Analyze operating premises which are the basis of impractical attempts, and show how they result in inadvertent and unwanted consequences.
2 Clarify How. Clarify how the client can more effectively get what she is after. Deal with objections, and clarify the risks involved.

VI. Instill New Patterns
1. Use Illustrations and Images. These may be used to introduce or clarify critical distinctions, and to maintain interest and avoid resistance.

2. Familiarize (Bring It Home). Support, restate, and deal with objections, so that the client may truly assimilate the information rather than merely hear it. Involve the client: have him try on more positive statements and practice new approaches.

3. Structure Carry-over. Promote the continuation of session gains into the client's everyday life. Make notes for the client to review. Have the client talk to family or friends about key insights, or include them in the sessions. Assign homework activities which maintain awareness of the suggested changes.

VII. Motivations

1. Appeal to What Matters. Values change slowly, and motivational changes in particular circumstances are made by appealing to what already matters to the client. Assess the client's motivations and values, and present what she needs to see or do in ways that make use of, rather than contradict, what counts. Show the client how what you are suggesting is a way to get what she really wants.

2. Avoid Generating Resistance. Resistance undermines cooperative collaboration. Coercion elicits resistance, and the occurrence of resistance means that the client sees the therapist as coercive (or pushy, unsympathetic, misguided). When resistance appears, look at what you are saying which the client sees as coercive. Re-describe information to make it acceptable, bypass objections, or leave the issue until later. When intentions are unacceptable, use outcome descriptions which specifically omit intentions.

Exceptions: Minimize resistance, unless using it paradoxically to motivate a constructive reaction.

References

Angell, R. Reasoning *and logic*. New York: Appleton-Century-Crofts, 1964.

Atkinson, D.R. and Carskaddon, G. A prestigious introduction, psychological jargon, and perceived counselor credibility. *Journal of Counseling Psychology*, 1975, 22, 180-186.

Brehm, S.S. The application of social psychology to clinical practice. Washington, D.C.: Hemisphere, 1976.

Corsini, R. and Contributors. *Current Psychotherapies* (2nd ed.). Itasca, Ill.: F.E. Peacock, 1979.

Davis, K.E. (Ed.). *Advances in Descriptive Psychology (Vol. 1)*. Greenwich, Conn.: JAI Press, 1981.

Dimond, R., Havens, R., and Jones, A. A conceptual framework for the practice of prescriptive eclecticism in psychotherapy. American Psychologist, 1978, 33, 239-248.

Driscoll, R (1981). Policies for pragmatic psychotherapy. In K.E. Davis (Ed.). Advances in Descriptive Psychology, Vol. I. Greenwich , Conn.: JAI Press, 273–276

Driscoll. R. and Edwards, L. The misconception of Christian suffering. Pastoral Psychology, 1983.

Farber, A. Castaneda's Don Juan as psychotherapist. In K.E. Davis (Ed.), Advances in Descriptive Psychology (Vol. 1). Greenwich, Conn: JAI Press, 1981.

Frank, J.D. Persuasion and healing. Baltimore: Johns Hopkins, 1961.

Frankl, V. Man's search for meaning: An introduction to logotherapy. New York: Washington Square Press, 1963.

Garfield, S. and Bergin, A. (Eds.). *Handbook of psychotherapy and behavior change (2nd ed.)*. New York: John Wiley and Sons, 1978.

Garfield, S. and Kurtz, R. Clinical psychologists in the 1970s. *American Psychologist*, 1976, 31, 1-9.

Ginott, H. *Between parent and child*. New York: Macmillan, 1965.

Goldfried, M. Toward the delineation of therapeutic change principles. *American Psychologist*, 1980, 35, 991-999.

Gordon, T. *Parent effectiveness training*. New York: Peter H. Wyden, 1970. Grier, W. and Cobbs, P. Black rage. New York: Bantam Books,

1968. Haley, J. *Strategies of psychotherapy*. New York: Grune & Stratton, 1963.

Haley, J. Approaches to family therapy. In J. Haley (Ed.), Changing families: A family therapy reader. New York: Grune & Stratton, 1971.

Haley, J. *Problem solving therapy*. San Francisco: Jossey-Bass, 1976.

Hall, C. and Lindzey, G. Theories of personality (2nd ed.). New York: John Wiley & Sons, 1970.

Hass, R.G. and Linder, D.E. Counterargument availability and the effects of message structure on persuasion. Journal of Personality and Social Psychology, 1972, 23, 219-233.

Heider, F. The psychology of interpersonal relations. New York: John Wiley and Sons, 1958.

Holmes, J. Psychotherapy: A means-ends study (LRI Report No. 5). Boulder, Colo.: Linguistic Research Institute, 1970.

Homme, L.E. Perspectives in psychology: XXIV. Control of coverants, the operants of the mind. Psychological Record, 1965, 15, 501-511.

James, W. The varieties of religious experience (Forward by J. Barzun). New York: New   American Library, 1958.

Jones, R.A. and Brehm, J. W. Persuasiveness of one- and two-sided communications as a function of awareness there are two sides. Journal of Experimental Social Psychology, 1970, 6, 47-56.

Kagan, J., Kearsley, R., and Zelazo, P. Infancy: Its place in human development. Cambridge, Mass.: Harvard University Press, 1978.

Kelly, E. L. Clinical psychology-1960. Report of survey findings. Newsletter: Division of Clinical Psychology of the American Psychological Association, 1961, 14 (1), 1-11.

Koch, S. (Ed.). Psychology: A study of a science (Vols. 1-6). New York: McGrawHill, 1959, 1962, 1963.

Kuhn, T.S. The structure of scientific revolutions (2nd ed.). Chicago: University of Chicago Press, 1970.

Landfield, A. and Leitner, L. (Eds.). Personal construct psychology. New York: John Wiley & Sons, 1980.

McWilliams, S.A. Eclecticism: Comprehension or jumble? A review of J. Palmer's A primer of eclectic psychotherapy. Contemporary Psychology, 1981, 26, 301.

Morris, C. Signs, language, and behavior. New York: George Braziller, 1955. Mowrer, O.H. Loss and recovery of community: A guide to the theory and practice of integrity therapy. In G.M. Gazda (Ed.), Theories and method of group psychotherapy and counseling. Springfield, Ill.: Charles C. Thomas, 1968.

Oppenheimer, J.R. Analogy in science. American Psychologist, 1956, 11, 127-136. Ossorio, P.G. Persons (LRI Report No. 3). Boulder, Colo.: Linguistic Research Institute, 1966.

Ossorio, P.G. Clinical topics (LRI Report No. 11). Boulder, Colo.: Linguistic Research Institute, 1976.

Ossorio, P.G. Meaning and symbolism (LRI Report No. 15). Boulder, Colo.: Linguistic Research Institute, 1978 (originally published in 1969).

Ossorio, P.G. Notes on behavior description. In K.E. Davis (Ed.), Advances in Descriptive Psychology (Vol. 1). Greenwich, Conn.: JAI Press, 1981 (originally published in 1969).

Ossorio, P.G. A multicultural psychology. In K.E. Davis and R. Bergner (Eds.), Advances in Descriptive Psychology (Vol. 3). Greenwich, Conn.: JAI Press, 1983 (in press).

Pepinsky, H.B. and Patton, M.J. Informative display and the psychological experiment. In H.B. Pepinsky and M.J. Patton (Eds.), The psychological experiment: a practical accomplishment. New York: Pergamon Press, 1971.

Pitkin, H. Wittgenstein and justice. Berkeley: University of California Press, 1972. Plotkin, W. Consciousness. In K.E. Davis (Ed.), Advances in Descriptive Psychology (Vol. 1). Greenwich, Conn.: JAI Press, 1981.

Ryle, G. The concept of mind. New York: Barnes and Noble, 1949.

Shontz, F. Research methods in personality. New York: Appleton-Century-Crofts, 1965.

Skinner, B.F. The behavior of organisms. New York: Appleton-Century-Crofts, 1938.

Sloane, R.B., Staples, F.R., Cristol, A.H., Yorkston, N.J., and Whipple, K. Psychotherapy versus behavior therapy. Cambridge, Mass.: Harvard University Press, 1975.

Smith, D. Trends in counseling and psychotherapy. American Psychologist, 1982, 37, 802-809.

Strong, S. R. Counseling: An interpersonal influence process. Journal of Counseling Psychology, 1968, 15, 215-224.

Strong, S. R. Social psychological approach to psychotherapy research. In S. Garfield and A. Bergin (Eds.), Handbook of psychotherapy and behavior change (2nd ed.). New York: John Wiley & Sons, 1978.

Strupp, H.H. Psychotherapy research and practice: An overview. In S. Garfield and A. Bergin (Eds.), Handbook of psychotherapy and behavior change (2nd ed.). New York: John Wiley and Sons, 1978.

Wachtel, P.L. Psychoanalysis and behavior therapy: Toward an integration. New York: Basic Books, 1977.

Wachtel, P.L. What should we say to our patients?: On the wording of therapists comments. Psychotherapy: Theory, Research, and Practice, 1980, 17, 183-188. Watts, A. Psychotherapy east and west. New York: New American Library, 1961. Wessler, R.A. and Wessler, R.L. The principles and practice of rational-emotive therapy. San Francisco: Jossey-Bass, 1980.

Whitehead, A.N. The aims of education and other essays. New York: New American Library, 1929.

Wilson, J. Thinking with concepts. Cambridge: Cambridge University Press, 1963. Wittgenstein, L. Philosophical investigations (trans. by G.E.M. Anscombe; 3rd ed.). New York: Macmillan, 1968.

Footnotes

---

1. See J. Norcross (1986) p.12 for brief summary of this research.

2. Wachtel, 1977; Sloane R.B., F.R., Staples, A.H. Cristol & J.J. Yorkson & K. Wipple (1975) *Psychotherapy Versus Behavior Therapy.* Cambridge: Harvard Universtiy Press; Swan, G.E. & M.L. Macdonald (1978) Behavior therapy in practice: A national survey of behavior therapists. *Behavior Therapy*, 9, 799-807. [cited in *JIEP* 5 2 180]

3. The number of separate schools of therapy was estimated at over 250 in 1980 (Corsini, 1981; Herink, 1980) and closer to 400 a mere six years later (T.B. Karasu, 1986) The specificity versus nonspecificity dilemma: Toward identifying therapeutic change agents. *American Journal of Psychiatry*, 143, 687-695.

4. 4.Cf. Sigmund Koch. (1981) The nature and limits of psychological knowledge: Lessons of a century qua "science." *American Psychologist*, 36, 257-269.

5. Similar to the "therapeutic underground" of common wisdom shared by clinicians but unrelated to theoretical schools, suggested by Paul Wachtel (1977).

6. Chomsky (1964) Review of Skinner's verbal behavior. In J.J. Katz & J.A. Fodor (Eds.), *The Structure of Language: Readings in the Philosophy of Language.* Englewood Cliffs, NJ: Prentice-Hall; Chomsky (1973), The case against B.F. Skinner. In F.W. Matson (Ed.), *Without Within: Behaviorism and Humanism.* Monterey, CA: Brooks/Cole.

7. The principal apologist for new languages himself recognized that the findings would be lost once a theoretical framework falls from favor. See: B.F. Skinner (1950) Are theories of learning necessary? *Psychological Review*, 57, 193-216.

8. J.C. Norcorss & B.L. Thomas (1988) What's stopping us now?: Obstacles to psychotherapy integration. *Journal of Integrative and Eclectic Psychotherapy*, 7, 74-80.

9. Cf. R. Driscoll (1988) A case against multiple languages for psychotherapists.

JIEP, 7, 3, 243-246.

1010.Barry E. Wolfe and Marvin Goldfried (1988). Research on psychotherapy integration: Recommendations and conclusions from an NIMH workshop. *Journal of Consulting and Clincial Psychology*, 3, 448-451.

1111.John D.W. Andrews. (1989) Integrative Languages in Therapeutic Practice and Training: Promises and Pitfalls. *JIEP*, 8, 4, (pages?).

1212.B.F. Skinner (1938) *The Behavior of Organisms*. New York: Appleton-Century-Crofts, p. 7.

1313.J. Austin (1957) A plea for excuses. *Proceedings of the Aristotelian Society*, 57, 1-30 (p. 8).

1414.See Fritz Heider, *The Psychology of Interpersonal Relations*. New York: Wiley, 1958.

1515.Probably the most readable summary of Ossorio is: Mary McDermott Shideler *Persons, Behavior, and the World: A Descriptive Psychology Approach.* (Lanham, Maryland: University Press of America, 1988)

1616.Steven Pinker (1997). *How the Mind Works*. NY: W.W. Norton.

1717.Peter Ossorio (1981) Notes on behavior description. In K.E. Davis (Ed.), *Advances in Descriptive Psychology* (Vol. 1). Greenwich, Conn: JAI Press.

1818.Eg. K.G. Shaver (1981) *Principles of Social Psychology* (2nd ed.). Cambridge, MA: Winthrop. [in Fletcher, 1984]

1919.B.F. Skinner (1978) *Reflections on behaviorism and society*. Englewood Cliffs, NJ: Prentice-Hall, p. 85.

2020.Garth Fletcher (1984) *American Psychologist*. Psychology and Common Sense. (39, 3, 203-213).

2121.Hall and Lindsay (1970) p.591. Italics in original.

2222.Fritz Heider (1958) p. 181.

2323.Peters, 1960, p. 155. [in Fletcher 1984]

2424.Alfred North Whitehead (1929, p.110)

2525.Oppenheimer is the father of the atomic bomb. J. Robert Oppenheimer

211

(1956, p.128)

26.Cited in Jensen and Tonies Software Engineering. [Joel Jeffrey will get complete citation.] (708) 653-0156

27.Cf. Sigmund Koch (1959) Epilogue. In S. Koch (Ed.) Psychology: A study of a science (Vol. 3). New York: McGraw-Hill.

28.A. Kaplan (1964) The Conduct of Inquiry: Methodology for Behavioral Sciences. San Francisco: Chandler.

29.Not counting air resistance. Illustration by Fred Driscoll.

30.This is a maxim in Peter Ossorio's conceptual formulations for behavior description. P.G. Ossorio (1981) Notes on behavior description. In K.E. Davis (Ed.), *Advances in Descriptive Psychology* (Vol. 1). Greenwich, Conn: JAI Press.

31.In ordinary speech we say that we know things, in the absence of absolute certainty. Cf. Pitkin (1972, p. 85-89).

32. In language analysis as in grammar, a paradigm case is to be used to convey the essential features of a phenomena. Peter Ossorio introduced the paradigm case formulation, parametric analysis, and transformational system used here to conceptualize behavior and its variations. P.G. Ossorio (1981) Conceptual-notational devices: the PCF and related types. In K.E. Davis (Ed.), *Advances in Descriptive Psychology (Vol.1)*. Greenwich, Conn: JAI Press. See also Wilson, 1963.

33. The paradigm case of human action is something done in order to bring about an end, according to R.S. Peters (1958) *The Concept of Motivation*. New York: Humanities Press (p. 4). Intentional action as the paradigm case of behavior is developed in P. Ossorio (1981). Notes on behavior description. In K.E. Davis (Ed.), *Advances in Descriptive Psychology (Vol. 1)*. Greenwich, Conn: JAI Press.

34. (1966)

35. cf. Plotkin, 1981.

36. Ossorio (1981)

37. attributed to media psychiatrist Frank Pittman.

212

38.38.The concept of technical eclecticism was introduced by Arnold Lazarus (1967) In support of technical eclecticism. *Psychological Reports* 21, 415-416.

39.39.Ludwig Wittgenstein (1968, par. 546)

40.40.R. Searle (1969) *Speech Acts*. Cambridge, England: Cambridge University Press.

41.41.J.F.T. Bugental (1987) *The Art of the Psychotherapist*. New York: W.W Norton.

42 Sloane et al. (1975)

43 (cf. Wachtel, 1980)

44 Strupp (1978)

45.cf. Strong, (1978).

46 Haim Ginott (1965),

47 Thomas Gordon (1970)

48 (cf. Hass and Linder, 1972; Jones and Brehm, 1970)

49 (cf. Angell, 1964)

50 (Driscoll and Edwards, 1983)

51 Ray Bergner.

52 (cf. Haley, 1971)

53 (cf. Landfield and Leitner, 1980)

54 cf Ossorio, 1976)

55 (cf. Ryle, 1949)

56.Wessler and Wessler (1980)

57 William Miller, and Stephen Rollnick 1991). Motivational Interviewing. New York, Guilford Press.

58 Driscoll, R (1981)